Beyond Termination

BEYOND TERMINATION

Myra Marshall
with Dan McGee, Ph.D.
Jennifer Bryon Owen

BROADMAN PRESS
NASHVILLE, TENNESSEE

© Copyright 1990 ● Broadman Press
All rights reserved
4260-15
ISBN: 0-8054-6015-2
Dewey Decimal Classification: 254
Subject Heading: CHURCH STAFF // MINISTERS // MINISTERS' FAMILIES
Library of Congress Catalog Card Number: 90-30949
Printed in the United States of America

Epistles reprinted from *Epistles/Now* by Leslie F. Brandt, Copyright © 1974, 1976 Concordia Publishing House, St. Louis. Reprinted by permission from CPH.

Scripture quotations marked NASB are from the *New American Standard Bible.* © The Lockman Foundation, 1960, 1962, 1963, 1968, 1971, 1972, 1973, 1975, 1977. Used by permission. Scripture quotations marked NIV are from the Holy Bible, *New International Version*, copyright © 1973, 1978, 1984 by International Bible Society. Used by permission. Verses marked TLB are taken from *The Living Bible.* Copyright © Tyndale House Publishers, Wheaton, Illinois, 1971. Used by permission.

Library of Congress Cataloging-in-Publication Data
Marshall, Myra, 1933-
        Beyond termination / Myra Marshall, Dan McGee, Jennifer Byron
Owen.
        p. cm.
        Includes bibliographical references.
        ISBN 0-8054-6015-2
        1. Marshall, Myra, 1933- . 2. Clergymen's wives--United States-
-Biography. 3. Baptists--United States--Biography. 4. Clergy-
-Dismissal of. 5. Southern Baptist Convention--Clergy.
6. Baptists--Clergy. 7. Married people in church work. 8. Wives-
-Effect of husband's employment on. I. McGee, Dan, 1939- .
II. Owen, Jennifer Byron, 1947- . III. Title.
BX6495.M3244A3 1990
253'.2—dc20
                                                                      90-30949
                                                                      CIP

To
Frank Marshall

Contents

Foreword

Beyond Termination is about surviving the traumas of a forced termination. Such an experience pulsates with pain and suffering. Survivors literally "walk through the valley of the shadow of death." It takes everything they can do, along with support from family and friends, to get beyond their valley of pain to the hillside of health and growth. This book records a minister's wife's courageous struggle to go beyond termination.

Myra was well on her way beyond the pain of termination when she and I met. As I listened to her story, it became obvious that the termination of her husband had almost destroyed her. I felt empathetic toward her for those moments when she had silently screamed for understanding, patience, and acceptance. I also admired her persevering spirit and willingness to be vulnerable in sharing her pilgrimage with others.

The idea for *Beyond Termination* was spawned in her compassionate desire to help others who experience a forced termination. This book fills an urgent need. Research reveals the scope of such need. Ministers are being terminated at the alarming rate of hundreds per month. Even though much has been written about the issue of forced termination, virtually nothing has been written about how to survive the aftermath of its pain and devastation. This book tells how.

Dan McGee, a psychotherapist and Myra's brother, gives an

insightful interpretation of Myra's pilgrimage. His unique contribution brings a healthy balance between the principles of psychology and biblical truth. Diagnostic helps are given to assist a person in understanding emotions, thought patterns, and behavioral responses to forced termination.

The value of this book is inestimable. A fellow sufferer can find in Myra a compassionate friend who can "weep with those who weep and rejoice with those who rejoice." The book, therapeutically, is a "cup of cold water" to those who thirst for understanding and acceptance.

It is an indirect counselor. If you have been terminated, it will help you. If you desire to help someone who has been terminated, read this book and pass it on.

Forced termination often causes a minister and his family to become disillusioned with God, the church, and their calling. This book addresses these kinds of spiritual questions.

Beyond Termination provides valuable help in understanding and coping with feelings. They are often ambivalent and controlling. Dr. McGee's critique of Myra's experience leaves no doubt that misunderstood and unattended emotional pain can make a person sick. This book provides insights for healing damages emotions.

"Is there a book I can give a terminated minister that will help him cope with being fired?" I was recently asked. My answer then was no. My answer now is yes. Thank you Myra for *Beyond Termination.* It will be to all forced termination sufferers an oasis of hope in a desert of rejection.

Norris Smith
Forced Termination Consultant
Sunday School Board of the
Southern Baptist Convention

Acknowledgments

Numerous people deserve public words of appreciation for their varied roles in birthing this book. I am grateful to the courageous women who shared their personal stories about forced termination in their own lives and to those people who assisted me in finding these women.

I owe thanks to a number of coworkers at the Baptist Sunday School Board: Norris Smith, who said in the planning stages of this book, "Don't give up" and who encouraged us all through it; Joe Richardson, who counseled me; to my manager for her patience and encouragement; and to Cheryl Beasley for her support and listening ear.

Appreciation also goes to the pastors and their wives Frank and I have had at Bellevue Baptist Church in Nashville, Tennessee: Dr. Randy and Janet Hyde; Dr. Michael and Grace Smith; and Dr. Kenny and Sherry Cooper. I am grateful to Bellevue Baptist Church and the choir for their acceptance, love, and support, and for providing us a healing place.

My thanks to Lela Hendrix for her professional guidance in developing the ideas for this book and for her friendship. My gratitude to Kyle Duvall for his generosity in sharing his knowledge and research. I am forever indebted to Dr. C. Ewing Cooley, the psychologist at Metro-McGee, who counseled me.

Finally, my deepest appreciation and gratitude to our families: to my husband, Frank, who believed enough in the mission of this book to not only allow, but to support, the revealing of our personal lives; to our son, Les, and his wife and to our daughter, Mydonna, and her husband for their openness and participation in the book; to Dan's wife, Sandra, who sacrificed their personal vacation time and who endured one more project on Dan's agenda, and to the staff at Metro-McGee who assumed additional responsibilities during this book's writing; to Jennifer's husband, John, for his encouragement and computer skills; and to their son, Jordan, for his patience while "Mom works on her book with Miss Myra."

This may well be one of the reasons our loving God
    permits suffering to afflict us;
      it keeps our heads straight and our hearts focused
    on the truly important goal of our lives,
    a right relationship with God.

2 Peter 1, Epistles/Now

Sufferings, trials, conflicts come to all of us
    at one time or another.
They cannot be avoided or ignored.
They are real—and they hurt.
But in addition to trusting God
    in the midst of conflicts,
      we can cushion their shock or lessen their hurt
      by holding on to one another, by loving, sharing,
      helping to bear one another's burdens and sufferings.
This is what it means to belong to the family of God.

—1 Peter 4, Epistles/Now

Introduction

Our adult son and daughter were "home," along with their families, for the Thanksgiving holidays, a rare and precious time for us. One evening the grandchildren were fast asleep, and the adults were sitting around the kitchen table, visiting.

Place is important to this story because the kitchen, specifically around the table, has always been the gathering spot for family discussions. This was especially true on Sunday nights after church when our children were growing up.

Those minutes and hours around that table provided the setting for family talk that ranged from playful joking to thoughtful, problem-solving and value-setting discussions.

The Marshall family is emotionally attached to our kitchen table. A lot of our life has been lived there. So you can imagine the fun we were having as we experienced this once again with our children, now married adults, and with their mates. This night was one of those wonderful, unhurried occasions when families enjoy being together and talking about whatever pops into someone's mind.

As usually happens, the conversation grew more serious as the hour grew later. Our son, Les, and our daughter, Mydonna, who are six years apart in age, began comparing the differences in their growing up years at home. Pursuing this topic, it became evident that I was the major difference in their lives.

My daughter said, "Les, you weren't here when Mother was so sick. You don't know the mother who was on the drugs. The silence. Her weakness in handling her role as a wife and mother. We all had our own set of problems, but we did not communicate to help each other the way we always had before. Mother just copped out."

Les responsed, "I'll always remember Mother by Daddy's side. Whatever Daddy's calling was, Mother was there . . . whether she wanted to be or not. She did it because that was her role. I never heard Mother complain, but I don't know if she would have done all those things on her own. She was a wife."

Both children are correct in their assessment of me. They each had a different mother. And, you could say they now have a third mother, for today I am neither of the women they described that night.

A crisis in our lives changed me from a woman who had, at one time, supported her husband and his ministry with little thought of herself into one who got through each day with the help of prescription drugs. The crisis: my husband was forced to resign, or forced to terminate as it is popularly called, his employment as a minister of music on a church staff.

This forced termination was, for me, the culmination of all the feelings I had experienced concerning my role as his helper—sometimes as an unpaid staff member—in his ministry. It shattered the foundations of the personal and professional self I had been for more than twenty years. It adversely affected my faith, my churchmanship, and all my relationships. My husband's forced termination as a church staff minister altered our lives, in a unique way, forever.

I am on the other side of that pain and suffering now. This book is about the journey that brought me to where I am today, about the "third mother" my children have. For I am now, in many ways, a new person. I am no longer the woman who submerged herself in her husband's ministry or in the calm fog of prescription drugs. I not only survived the crisis, I also grew through it.

A situation such as the one I have been through may be a surprise to some of you. You and your family may never have been forced to leave a church staff position. Wonderful! I hope you never do. But, you will find this book helpful in understanding and helping your friends who do find themselves victims of forced termination—and you will have some. They will need your support and help more than you can ever imagine.

Also, reading this book may cause you to reevaluate your own role and ministry. Something in these pages might help you deal more effectively with a forced termination should it happen to you. You may find, too, some words that will help you have a more effective and satisfying ministry.

Unfortunately, others of you have experienced a situation similar to mine. In fact, you know exactly what I'm talking about. Some things in my story are unique to me; there are others you and I share. Your forced termination may not be complicated by a physical illness, as was mine. But, you may have some problem of another nature that complicates and is complicated by the termination crisis. Most likely you are searching for any clues to help you cope with your own plight.

Although you may be in a great deal of pain, I offer you not only sympathy, but also hope. You can survive. You can grow and even have a fuller and more rewarding life than before. I pray my experience will help you.

Let me acknowledge at this point that not all ministers are men and all spouses women. Increasingly, women are ministers employed on church staffs. Because of the thinking and practice in much of today's society, some of the problems encountered in forced termination will be different if the minister is a woman and the spouse is a man. However, some of the problems will be the same in that relationship.

Because in my case the spouse is a female, I am writing this book from my perspective and will use terminology that corresponds to my own situation. But, the essence of the book will be helpful to male and female spouses of terminated ministers, as well as unmarried ministers and even people who are not clergy but who are in a crisis.

One of the worst things about our forced termination was the feeling that I was all alone. Only much later did I discover that I was not. Increasing numbers of wives are being affected when their husbands are forced to terminate their church staff positions. My deepest appreciation goes to all the women who courageously shared their stories with me so that we might better help you. Their names have been changed, but you will find some of their most personal hurts, frustrations, and joys in these pages. You will find feelings and experiences similar, if not a mirror image, to your own.

I am sharing with you things I have learned experientially. Because I am not a trained counselor or theologian, I am not treating this matter from those perspectives. I am a layperson who experienced these things while stumbling in the darkness, yet seeing more light all along the way.

However, in these pages, I am sharing with you the love and insight of my brother Dan, who is a psychotherapist. His brotherly love, coupled with his professional insights and skills, supported me through this crisis.

A letter I received from Dan is indicative of the love and support he has so freely given me through the years:

> I am proud to be your brother. I've loved and admired you from birth. Nothing felt better than those frequent comments: "You look just like Myra."
> We also have other things in common. We know pain. We

know about struggle. We know about God's love. We have strong determination and have inherited the will to survive and wring the most out of life.

These are the kinds of things that make me believe we are indeed "made in His image." These are the things that will see you through the present struggle.

Real change is painful. If you take your therapy seriously, it will "smart" more than a little. But on the other side of the fearsome pain comes peace and a calm not unlike the birth of a baby. Life is full of pain so you might as well hurt constructively and have a worthy goal in mind. And it's pain that makes happiness meaningful.

As a psychotherapist in private practice who has also served eighteen years on a church staff, my brother is providing specific, professional guidance in this book. He well understands church life and one's commitment to it.

You must know two things about this book. It is not a "they lived happily after" story. Never do I want to give you the impression that I have all the answers, that I have arrived, or that I am glibly telling you what to do. On the contrary, life in the wake of forced termination still has its problems, and I struggle with them. But, I do feel better able to handle my problems. There are no quick fixes and no easy answers, but help is available.

The other point I must emphasize is that writing this book has not been easy for me or my family. We are private people, especially my husband, and, after all, he was the one who was forced to leave a job he loved.

A desire for my agony and pain to ultimately have meaning for myself, and perhaps for others, led me to undertake this project. However, I had second thoughts when putting pen to paper brought back the whole experience as fresh as if it were yesterday. I realized how open, how exposed, our lives will be to anyone who reads this book.

You see, we still live in the same city. I am employed in the major denominational institution in which I worked when the forced termination occurred and while I was so sick and dependent on prescription drugs. Many, many of my fellow employees did not know anything about our situation at the time. Now, with my most private thoughts and feelings recorded on paper, they will. Members of the church we were forced to leave will now know how badly we hurt. People who did not know us at all will now know us almost as well as they would have had they been living in our home.

I deliberated at length about whether or not I wanted to allow myself and family to become so vulnerable, to have my most personal feelings and weaknesses in black and white for anyone to see.

So, why am I telling you all of this? Since I discovered that my husband is not the only person ever forced to terminate his position on a church staff and I am not the only spouse for whom this experience was devastating, I have wanted to help others. I would like for my experience to produce something of value, not only for myself, but for others. Sharing this with you may be one of the "worthy goals," as Dan mentioned in his letter to me, which evolved from the hurt. Perhaps this will give more meaning to my experience.

Although you would not choose this path, beauty and growth can flower from all your pain. I am telling you my story to encourage you, to testify that you, too, can reach the other side.

Be assured there is someone who knows your pain and who cares, because I do. I wish I could put my arms around each one of you who are hurting and tell you that I understand and I care. This book is my way of doing that.

Myra Marshall

We need not pray that God remove our painful experiences,
but that He transform them into cleansing fires that
renew and refurbish us for His purposes,
and that we always remain faithful to Him.
—2 Timothy 2, *Epistles/Now*

1
Forced Termination
Invades Our Lives

"I just wanted to tell you I'm going to resign Sunday," my husband said in his direct, matter-of-fact manner when he called our daughter and me into the den one night several years ago.

Simple words. Easy to understand—at least on the surface. Yet the full meaning of these words would create havoc in our lives for years to come. And, although their edge is not quite as sharp now, hardly a day goes by in which we don't remember them and the way they shredded our lives.

My husband, Frank, was resigning as minister of music on the staff of a three-thousand-plus member church, a position he had held for eight years.

On this particular night we discussed—rather calmly, given the significance of Frank's announcement—the decision and our future. The shock, the real problems, the engulfing feelings would come later. The magnitude of being forced to terminate, having to leave, had not hit us yet. But, it would batter us repeatedly for the next few years. For you see, my husband's decision and the subsequent events was one of the most devastating experiences I had ever encountered.

Although it may have seemed so to many of the church members, the decision to resign from the church was not of my husband's own making. The following Sunday, while Frank and I listened from the hall and our daughter sat in the back of the sanctuary, the chairman of the deacons read Frank's letter of resignation. But, resigning was not our choice.

Clues that his decision was not really what Frank wanted or planned at this time were evident. He announced no plans to move to another church staff; no reason was given for his departure; and it all happened very suddenly and unexpectedly.

My husband was a victim of what, in church circles, is called forced termination. I prefer calling this process forced resignation. Because of the way this process is handled in most churches, it looks as if it is a normal resignation, a departure of one's own choosing. But it is not. The victim resigns under pressure, is forced to end his work with that particular church and to leave. He has been terminated, but to make things look better, perhaps more "Christian," it is called a resignation.

Frank had no desire to leave this church at this time. In fact, for the previous year our church had been without a pastor, and opportunities to join several other church staffs had presented themselves to us. But, Frank had wanted to stay. He felt the church needed him. At the time of the resignation, he was the only full-time staff minister. Much of the responsibility for carrying on the duties normally assigned to other staff people, from hospital visitation to answering burglar alarm calls in the middle of the night, had fallen to him. He did these things because he wanted to do them. This was where we felt God had called us to minister, and this was where we wanted to be.

However, other human beings made decisions for us that contradicted what we felt to be God's leadership for our lives. Going into all the details and particular history about our own forced termination is not appropriate here. I must say some things, however, to let you know the magnitude of our hurt and to reassure you that there are people who understand exactly what you are going through. I have found our experience to be very similar to that of many other couples who have been forced to terminate from their churches.

Some situations demand that a staff minister be terminated. Of course, I don't think our termination was justified, and I don't think it was conducted appropriately. Based on my conversations with others, I've learned that few forced terminations are handled well, or even as well as they could be, given the delicate situation of forced termination.

One thing I want to make very clear is that the purpose of this book is not to fight some sort of battle with churches that have terminated staff ministers. We have not identified any church in this book. Any details about the actual termination are included in this book only to explain what is being said. We do not want to embarrass anyone. We are seeking to help both churches and ministers understand the effects of termination on the minister and his family.

In our case, a prospective pastor was coming to the church soon "in view of a call," to be considered by the congregation to fill the position of senior minister. According to the chairman of the governing body, the person in the church who approached my husband about terminating, the prospective pastor wanted to name his own staff. Our resignation was wanted before this new man came to the church. The person relating this to my husband demanded Frank's resignation.

Although deeply hurt, with a hurt that will never leave entirely, my husband complied with this demand. His response was the same many ministers have given when confronted with the same situation. My husband's response was, "The church is bigger than I am, so I'll just move on."

He would leave quietly. He did not want to do anything to hurt the church. We've found that most staff ministers don't want to "take sides," to "stand up for themselves," or to risk embroiling the church in controversy because they do not want to hurt the church.

But, just moving on is not as simple as it sounds. Being asked to leave immediately is far different from the staff minister's own journey taking him somewhere. Being asked to leave, for whatever reason, is devastating to one's self-esteem. Being asked to leave immediately throws one into a frantic scramble just to meet the daily demands of living.

Being asked to leave your job on a church staff calls into question everything you have ever believed about God, His will for your life, and His leadership. People are terminated from their jobs all the time. Heads of corporations are fired when businesses fail. Reorganizations within companies leave employees without jobs. Mismanagement and misconduct cause people to be terminated from jobs. People employed in the secular world lose their jobs unjustly and without good reason.

While the losses experienced in being terminated from a secular job are not to be trivialized, being forced to terminate from a church staff position has another aspect that makes the burden even heavier. When one is employed by a church, the place where one works is also the place where one worships. The place where we worked was intimately tied into our relationship to God and His people. It was meshed with our calling, purpose, and direction in life. And the church, or certain ones in the church, did not want us, so it seemed to me.

The effects of forced termination were not felt only by my husband. It affected me to the core of my personhood and was the culmination of a lifetime of experiences and feelings about being involved in church work.

For me, and for other women in the same situation with whom I've talked, forced termination does not happen in a vacuum. It is not an isolated incident. Forced termination affects every area of one's life. It even calls up emotions and needs from one's past; feelings and hurts from past encounters with people and situations closest to us. Problems that one thinks have been conquered, or at least handled, rush fiercely to the forefront. When new wounds are inflicted, old ones open and bleed afresh.

Relief was the first feeling I had after Frank told me of his decision. The pressures of being intricately involved in church work had weighed heavily on me all my life, and I was relieved at not having to feel this pressure anymore. My husband has later said that I had been under stress for such a long time that any change probably would have had a positive effect on me. But, the positive effects of this change were a long time in coming.

I've learned that I had not developed adequate coping skills for dealing with life's problems. So, the pressures of stress had been building over an entire lifetime, a lifetime in which I expected a great deal of myself. As the oldest child in a pastor's family, I experienced a lot of things unique to the first child.

At twenty-two years of age, I married a man committed to ministering to others through a church. My talents were also in the field of music, so I used them to help my husband in his work. As did many women of my generation, I often became an unpaid church staff member. I sang in my husband's choirs. I played the organ or the piano. I led children's choirs. And, as my son said, I even sang with Frank so that all of his special music did not have to be solos!

Our home was always open for entertaining and helping people. While doing all this, I was writing and leading conferences for various groups in our denomination. Some of these things I did because I wanted to do them. They were a part of what I felt to be my personal Christian calling.

Some of the things I did because I thought Frank needed my help, especially in the early days of his ministry. Unfortunately, some of my church-related activities were done because I felt I ought to do them. Our son says he was not aware when I crossed the line between wanting to do them and feeling I ought to do them. I'm not sure I know either, but that I had done so became obvious.

Handling the stresses that inevitably are involved in church work was not one of the things I did well. Naturally, when my husband was terminated from a job in which I had fully participated, the stress on me increased considerably. This seemed to be the culmination of problems that had been rumbling near the surface for years.

My reactions to the difficult part of church employment had begun much earlier in other churches, mainly because of the high expectations I put on myself and because of the times when God's people acted as if they belonged to someone else.

Lest I mislead you, everything in church was not bad, disagreeable, negative, or unhappy for us. Many good, kind, loving people were committed to serving the Lord through the churches we have served. We have had wonderful experiences worshiping and growing spiritually with these churches. But, as in most churches, there were some problems, some people who were not Christlike in their relationships to others. This was the part I had difficulty handling. With the forced termination, I would not have to continue trying to handle the stress this created. Little did I realize I was just swapping one object of stress for another.

My physical health had already begun to deteriorate before we joined this church staff. Shortly after we arrived in town, I had gone to a doctor who said my problems were not physical. He suggested I see a psychiatrist, an idea my husband emphatically vetoed. Frank has never believed nonchurch members should know about any negative inner workings of the church. Also he did not feel a non-Christian psychiatrist could understand our life orientation, which is based on Christianity.

The doctor also prescribed a tranquilizer. Repeated visits to several doctors yielded a similar diagnosis and more prescriptions for tranquilizers.

So I had the perfect out, so to speak, when the immediate stage of relief over the forced termination ended, as it was sure to do, and the acute feelings started—feelings of embarrassment at being fired; anger at those who did the firing, at those who did nothing to stop them, and at God; hurt caused by those same people; bewilderment at how something like this could happen to us in a Christian institution; and fear for our future.

My symptoms were real. I truly was sick. But, for a long time I accepted the doctor's diagnosis, believing that it was all psychosomatic.[1] I later learned what the doctor meant by the word *psychosomatic*, but at the time my understanding of his diagnosis only made me feel worse.

Feeling weak and incompetent, I was ashamed that I couldn't handle myself and the negative forces in my life any better than I apparently seemed to be doing. The physical symptoms of illness were real. Whatever the cause, they were present in the form of severe headaches and stomach problems. And I suffered from them. In an attempt to abate the pain, I took prescription drugs that doctors had given me.

When the dark storm clouds of forced termination engulfed me, my physical symptoms worsened. I took more medicine. I didn't want to feel, so I didn't. Much of what happened in the months that followed is, literally, a blur. Many things are lost to me forever. I simply was not aware of a lot of what went on in our lives. So sick and on so many prescription drugs, I really couldn't care about anybody else's problems. And I certainly didn't want to care about my own.

I was well on my way to becoming a drug addict. This fact frightens me, even today, but it is true. I know because of the way I acted, manifesting many of the attitudes and actions of people who are addicted to drugs. At work I was careful not to let people know about all the tranquilizers I was taking, carefully controlling the amount I took during the workday. One painkiller I saved for nights and weekends because it produced such strange side effects and sensations. Strange side effects and sensations were not what I was seeking. Becoming numb to the physical and emotional pain was what I wanted, the only way I knew to deal with the problem.

I didn't want Frank to know how much medicine I was taking and, in reality, he didn't want to know either. When things were at their worst, he was traveling a lot in his new job (finally!), and it was easier for him to ignore the type and quantity of medication I was taking and its effect on me. But, he could not ignore, according to him, that I was becoming someone other than the person he had married. He has since said only that I was taking more drugs than he liked for me to.

Also during this time, the mother-daughter roles reversed, and our sixteen-year-old daughter became the one who took care of me when I was in such a fog that I could not manage. She knows all the stories, some of which would be funny if the situation had not been so grave, about my strange behavior when I didn't know what I was doing. Things I don't remember at all.

I also came close to involving another family in our problems—that of our son who lived in another state with his wife and children. He later told us that if he had known the full extent of what we were going through, he would have had to move near us in order to help. How grateful I am that my illness did not disrupt their family life in addition to our own.

Although I did not know it at the time, two barriers were blocking my path to dealing with our crisis of forced termination. I was physically ill, and that was to be proven later. A person needs to be in good physical condition in order to deal properly with any crisis. Also, I was using an artificial means to escape, a method that would increasingly make me dependent on it. Rather than solving problems, the escape offered by pre-scription drugs was creating more.

All times in our home were not bad. But, they were far from what they had been or what they could be. Life was becoming increasingly difficult. Somehow this situation made an impression on me. I thank God that enough of the "old Myra" was left to enable me to see things as they were and to realize our current life-style was not what I wanted for myself and our family.

My husband and daughter were hurting, too. Why should I be so selfish to think that I hurt any more than they did? And I was adding another hurt, another burden, to them. I did not want that. I did not want to be sick, to have to depend on prescription drugs to get through the day. I did not like the feelings of being a weak person.

Being a person of strength was what I really wanted. I wanted to be a person who was whole so that I could offer strength and support to my husband and daughter.

I suppose those desires had not been dimmed by the pain and drugs. At least, some of the time, I was able to look rationally at our home and our family life and decide how I wanted to be. I've always been a survivor and a fighter, especially if I thought I could do something to change things. My brother continually reminded me of this survival characteristic, of the tough times I had conquered already. I began to hold on to this belief.

My husband was also a strong force in leading me to be whole. I watched Frank and saw how he forgave. His Christlike attitude impressed me significantly. After all, he was the one who was terminated! I thought, *If he can do it, I can do it.* My thread of hope in this crisis was that I thought I could change.

Even after Frank found employment, and especially after we went to another church on a part-time basis, my stomach problems increased. I went to another doctor who confirmed that I did, indeed, have a physical problem and a pretty serious one at that. Adhesions resulting from ulcers had closed most of my stomach. My doctor was surprised that I could get even a drink of water into my stomach.

Repeatedly, the doctor told me, "Don't be so hard on yourself. You really are sick." My illness was not "in my head!" I was not imagining all that I had been through! That alone did wonders for my self-esteem.

Eventually, I learned more about the relationship between my physical problems and stress. My brother explained that while all physical symptoms do not result from stress, all people have certain medical and physical weaknesses. Stress intensifies these weaknesses.

Surgery to remove a major portion of my stomach was required, and the doctor told me that before it was all over I would wish I could die. He spoke the truth. Surgery and recovery were extremely painful.

However, as in many of the bad experiences of life, something good came out of this one. In order to undergo surgery, I had to quit taking the prescription drugs.

The first week after I returned home from the hospital, friends made the customary calls and visits to the sick. Then no one came to see me; I was left totally alone. At first I felt sorry for myself, but as time passed that total solitude proved to be a blessing.

The pain was awful and my recovery difficult. Consumed by that, my mind could not think about the forced termination. So, I did nothing. But, I wanted to get well so badly that the survival instinct took over. Any energy I had was directed toward wellness. My recovery time was a time of God teaching me to be still and be quiet. I could sit for hours and be peaceful, a feeling I had never had before.

Without any pressures, I could begin to deal with what had happened to us. While I was healing physically, emotional and spiritual healing began to take place.

Three months after surgery, I returned to work—a miracle in itself. According to my doctor, many people who have this kind of surgery never return to work at all. Several years passed, however, before the healing of my spirit was as complete.

The realization that spiritual healing had occurred came to me, almost suddenly, while I was accompanying my husband on a business trip. We were traveling toward the Great Smoky Mountains in East Tennessee. Not talking about anything in particular, we had been basking in the silence for a while. It was a quiet, peaceful trip, and I was enjoying the wonderful scenery. The sun and clouds were playing around the mountaintops as we crossed over and around the mountains. Blooming dogwood trees dotted the landscape. Inhaling these ideal surroundings, I became aware of a strange sense of God's presence with me.

It was almost as if He said aloud, "Myra, you are on the other side of all the old feelings about yourself and the others involved in this change in your lives." I felt a peace and a calmness about everything that I had worked toward for six years. I knew the words of the Still Small Voice were true.

Words of my brother also came quickly to mind. "One day you will suddenly notice you have turned a corner and you are doing things you thought you could never do." How right he was!

No longer was I the woman who subverted her own identity to that of her husband's career. Nor was I the physically and spiritually ill woman who gave herself up to the oblivion of prescription drugs.

I was a new person. My children really did have a third mother. I was a person who felt good about herself, one who had a more mature faith, and one who participated in church because she wanted to do so. I had learned a great deal about God, myself, other people, and how we all relate to each other.

I savored that experience between God and me, not even sharing it with Frank until later. I wanted to be sure of myself and my feelings, but I do know that point was when I became aware of truly being on my way to wholeness.

Climbing the mountain created by that forced termination did not happen overnight. Please understand this "mountain-top experience" was not arrival. It was the definite turn in my attitude and awareness that I had worked toward for so long. This realization was one of those wonderful times when I saw and felt the results of my self-talk, visualization, dreams, prayers, and much support from others who love me.

Reaching this point took several years, years of dealing daily with the problems, years of stepping carefully along life's path. I was not fully aware that I was getting to the other side while it was happening. Getting there was not easy. Our lives were difficult at times. We hurt. We don't, even today, have definite, easy answers to all the problems caused by forced termination. But, we are the overcomers instead of being overcome. And, I learned some things along the way.

My recovery was not a solitary endeavor. Help came to me from a variety of places. I know now that God put some wonderful, knowledgeable, and committed people in my path to recovery, and I shall be ever grateful for them. My purpose in this book is to share that help with you. Your experience of forced termination and your reaction to it will not be just like mine. The helps and solutions to my problems may not be exactly what you need to survive and overcome yours. However, there may be bits and pieces of insight that will comfort and guide you on your journey of working through the crises of forced termination.

I am on the other side. You can be, too. The aftermath of forced termination will pass, but you do have to work hard to help it pass. People frequently think healing is magic. Once the source of the pain is identified, it will go away and everything will be the way it once was, or so they think. Not so. The excruciating pain will go away, but not magically. Every day you live you will have to acknowledge that the forced termination is in the past and that you intend to keep it there.

I am telling you the same thing Dan told me and that I have repeated to myself many times: You have a life to live. How do you want to live it? The effects of forced termination are like a sickness I had to get out of myself. Each person, thought, song; each time I looked at my husband and children—anything that reminded me of our experience—I had to consciously decide how I would respond.

Making the decision about how I wanted to live the rest of my life was the first step, and a major one, in a journey up a steep, rocky mountain.

Dan's Observations

As Myra's brother and confidant, I feel uniquely qualified to comment, not only on her forced termination experience, but also on the impact of her childhood on her adult life.

A rare person reaches adult life perfectly equipped to handle the big crises of adulthood. All people have gaps in their childhood development, leaving them ill-equipped for handling certain kinds of crises. Myra was no exception.

While the events of forced termination in Myra and Frank's life would have had a major and serious impact on anyone, certain factors in Myra's background affected the impact of forced termination on her.

Myra was the firstborn in a pastor's family. Four more of us were to follow. She was born into the post-Depression Deep

South, where few people had anything, and those who did feared losing it again.

Myra's experience as the firstborn parallels that of most first-borns. With their first child, most parents are afraid they won't do it right, so they tend to overkill. They expect too much.

Therefore, the first child is frequently a highly performance-oriented, perfectionistic person. These traits are accompanied by some degree of rejection anxiety.

In Myra's case, these conditions produced an adult who is extremely talented. There is no doubt that all of her siblings would vote her the most talented of us all. And the perfection-ism, anxiety, and fear of rejection helped produce some of that talent.

One would think that success, accomplishing something sig-nificant, would resolve this anxiety. But, if the insecurity is deep enough, and I believe Myra's was, all of the accomplishments meant nothing. We all take pride in her skills, but Myra always showed discomfort with praise and discounted all compliments.

Myra continued to hold up a model of perfection that was totally unachievable by anyone. Therefore, she couldn't enjoy her success and always felt herself compared to someone else who was better. And there is always someone better, no matter who you are.

These insecurities produced a great deal of stress whenever Myra encountered problems of any magnitude. And let's re-member the historical setting here. Our society has been in a serious and soul-searching struggle regarding the role of women in the family, the work world, and the church. Many women of Myra's generation had no other option than to find their identity solely in the role of their husband's position in the community. Self-esteem rose and fell with the ups and downs of the spouse's career.

While we all hurt deeply when our spouses suffer, it is important for everyone to have a sense of accomplishment and achievement separate and apart from those of our partner, even as we offer support to them in stressful times. Research and clinical experience have shown that children do not fare well when the mother's identity is fused with or lost in that of the father's. Such conditions do not allow a person to develop the coping skills that come from personally overcoming obstacles.

I really don't think Myra had adequate coping skills going into the forced termination. Faced with the loss of her husband's job, the reasonable concern over financial security paled when compared to her loss of identity. As the reader will discover, with one great stroke, this forced termination robbed Myra Marshall of her identity as her husband's associate, as a church member and, for a while, her identity as a child of God.

Another way to test whether or not our faith is genuine
    is to see whether we can be thankful in the midst of
    trying circumstances.
Some of us suffer much in the course of our lives.
All of us are continually exposed to temptations
    and tribulations that are more than we can endure.
What we must understand is that God is able to use
    even these things,
        the apparently unfortunate happenings that hound us,
    to accomplish His purposes in and through us.
                            —1 Peter 1, *Epistles/Now*

2
I Discover I'm Not Alone

Alone. After we were terminated, I felt so totally alone. At times, the feeling was almost overwhelming.

Much of the life I had shared with other people had been taken from me, and I no longer connected with them in our common purpose. Also, the new arena into which I had been deposited was an unfamiliar one to me.

That one could be forced to leave the employment of a church was certainly a revelation to me. I had never known any others who had been forced to leave their church. I had only heard of ministers who had to leave because of wrongdoing. I didn't know it could happen to people who were doing their jobs and who were moral. And because of this, I thought this new status thrust on us was rare in clergy circles.

In the intervening years, I've learned differently. We were not alone. Many, many people have experienced, and are right now experiencing, forced termination. The termination of pastors seems to receive more attention, but it can and does happen to any minister on a church staff.

I am not the only person who wandered around, fearful and disconnected, in her aloneness. As I researched this book, I discovered many women who confirmed that this sense of being alone is a common feeling.

Some of these women cried freely while revealing their particular story to me. I was the first person with whom they could really be open and honest because each had thought she was the only one to experience this trauma. They too had not known anyone else who had experienced forced termination and, thereby, could really understand their feelings and needs.

Listen to what one terminated minister said. "The feeling of rejection and failure is almost incomprehensible. Why, if God is on his throne, could he allow his servants to be treated this way? That was the question I mulled over in my mind night after night. I felt so alone and defeated. I took it out on my family by being inconsistent and moody—they didn't deserve this treatment either."[1]

Forced termination situations usually are "kept quiet" by almost everyone involved. The silence has its reasons.

One minister gives us a clue. "I was the victim of an unjustified forced termination. It was the most cruel, horrifying, sickening and detestable ordeal of my life. Should I live a thousand years, I would never forget the nightmare of it or cease hurting from it."[2]

Embarrassment, such as that expressed by this minister, is one reason those who have been terminated feel alone. Losing one's job is, for most people, a humiliating experience. This happens to people in all areas of life, even striking those in highly visible places. Former President and Mrs. Carter have chronicled their own experience of not being reelected for a second term to our nation's highest office in 1980. They openly share their hurt and confusion over having to leave a job against their will and how they dealt with it. Their book *Everything to Gain, Making the Most of the Rest of Your Life* is an excellent story by two Christians who overcame perhaps the most public forced termination in our land and who now are leading fulfilling lives.

No one is immune to forced termination, and always in any situation the cloud of doubt hangs over the one terminated.

You fear people suspect that you failed, that you did something wrong, that you deserved to lose your job. Not only do you fear that others think these things, but you too begin to wonder if they might be true.

People seem to perceive being terminated from a church position differently than losing a secular job. The church's spiritual dimension adds a variable not found in most other jobs. Society places churches above this sort of thing. Therefore, to be fired from a church can be seen as the result of a very serious "sin." No matter what the circumstances, these factors lead to the embarrassment that perpetuates the silence surrounding forced termination.

Frequently, people forced to terminate remain quiet about what has happened because they do not "want to hurt the church." How many times I heard that as other women shared their stories for this book. Because of the nature of the church, its purpose, and its overall well-being, people do not want to challenge those who call for the termination.

Most church members usually do not know what has transpired, other than that a staff member has resigned. Since these people were not a part of the original decision to demand the resignation, those forced to resign think it better not to bring them in after the fact. Many forced termination victims feel it is better not to pursue righting the injustice (real or imagined), which could possibly involve the church in a controversy and which could sidetrack it from its mission.

My husband, Frank, felt this way. He was one of those who left quietly because he felt the church was bigger than he was. He did not want to hurt the church.

We have talked with victims of forced termination who did challenge the termination, who did speak to make their case known. Some even used legal means. However, this route is rare. It seems that most people remain silent.

If the termination has not been handled properly or if it is unjustified, those in the church who call for the resignation may want to keep the incident a secret. They do not want their actions scrutinized or opened up to public opinion. Frequently, the call for resignation is made by only a small number of people within the church, without total church knowledge or action.

Sometimes, when termination of a church staff employee is necessary, it is handled as quietly as possible so it will not embarrass the staff member and his family. While this is commendable and understandable in these cases, when all terminations are secret, the cloak of wrongdoing embraces the innocent ones as well.

Another reason for feeling so alone is that forced termination seems to carry with it "guilt by association." People have told me how they were ostracized by other staff members, by other ministers and paid staff people in their denomination. It seems these former associates did not know what to say or how to help. Perhaps they felt their own positions would be in jeopardy if they continued their relationships with the terminated. Perhaps they were afraid.

Also, the people who do know about your crisis and who love you may not be equipped to help or may not adequately understand. We will talk more about this in another chapter. Suffice it to say here that you may have many people who love you but who cannot help. This only intensifies your aloneness.

Whatever the reasons, the silence creates an atmosphere in which each terminated person feels he is the only one who has had this experience. Only after I began to heal physically and spiritually did I discover that, indeed, I was not alone. As I recovered, I was able to look at the total situation of forced termination and consider what it meant, not just to me personally, but also to others in church work.

Gradually, Frank and I began meeting other people or hearing about other staff members who had been through similar experiences. Several months after our termination Frank took a secular job that required he travel and call on churches, as well as other institutions. While doing this, he has become acquainted with people who have been forced to terminate.

In fact, Frank now has a file of resumes given to him by people he meets through his travels. Many of them are from ministers who, sometimes overtly but most often subtly, are being forced out.

We have met others, in unusual and mysterious ways, who have been forced to terminate. One Sunday morning, I was setting up my music at the organ in preparation for the upcoming service. Frank motioned for me to come to the other side of the sanctuary where he was standing with two men whom I did not know. He had not known these men, who were visiting in our church, but greeted them when they arrived for worship services. Frank introduced me to them, saying they were pastors from a distant state, and both of them had been terminated from their pastorates. They were in our city to attend a forced termination seminar that was to begin the next morning.

When I asked how they chose our church, they responded, "The Yellow Pages." We took them to lunch following our service and spent the afternoon listening to the agony of their experiences. They were so touched by having someone who understood and with whom they could talk that they came by my office the next day to tell me again of their appreciation.

As time passed, we talked with enough people like these men to convince us that ours was not an isolated incident. Indeed, forced termination seemed to be all too common, not only in our denomination, but others as well. So many, many people are like those two men we met at our church. They need understanding, concern, and help.

Forced terminations, according to Brooks Faulkner, are not limited to one denomination or group of people. Says Faulkner in his book, *Forced Termination*:

> Unfortunately, this happening is not unusual. It is happening among Baptists, Methodists, Presbyterians, Episcopalians, Church of the Brethren, Christian churches, and every denomination in the United States—even the world. Some have called it an "epidemic." Perhaps it is no better or worse than it has been in the past, but it appears to be worse. Ministers appear to be more willing to talk about the pain and humiliation of being fired or forced to resign.[3]

Although we met enough people and heard enough stories to know for ourselves that forced termination is a growing problem in church life, proving this factually and statistically is difficult. The lack of a large body of widely known, factual information also contributes to the isolation felt by those to whom forced termination happens.

Most denominations do not keep records on this sort of thing. Although our book is not intended to be a scientific study, we contacted a number of denominational headquarters for their own statistics on forced termination. Most responded that forced termination did not occur in that denomination or that, if it did, they had no record of its frequency. Most denominations have no records that tell why a person leaves a church. For the most part, they are not aware forced termination is a problem. In fact, only in the last few years have any denominations acknowledged forced termination and the need to provide help for both the one terminated and for the church.

We have found only a few studies that deal, directly or indirectly, with forced termination. However, those have been quite revealing in showing the depth of hurt that results from forced termination and the seriousness of the problem.

Now, you may hear the words *research* and *statistics* and decide to skip to the next chapter. But, please don't. Stay with me. Remember that each statistic represents a real person who hurts and struggles just as you and I do.

While these research projects cover a variety of facets of forced termination, we will point out primarily those things that deal with the spouse and family, since that is the focus of our book.

Dr. Louis Ball, chairman of the Division of Fine Arts at Carson-Newman College in Jefferson City, Tennessee, conducted one of the first studies I found that indicates the pervasiveness of forced termination. "A Study of Tenure for the Minister of Music at a Time of Pastoral Change" reveals that ministers of music are more fearful and insecure about their positions at a time of pastoral change than at any other time.

This transition in a church does seem to be a frequent cause of forced termination. A new pastor comes on the scene and wants to build his own staff, and so he "cleans house."

In his findings, Ball determined that there were several long-term detrimental or beneficial effects of forced termination and one of these dealt with the effects on the family. These personal statements by his respondents were what really gripped my heart when I read them.

> . . . the trauma was very difficult on my family.
> . . . family now goes to church very little. Wife has never recovered.
> . . . marriage has ended, due, at least in part, to the church termination.
> Devastating to my wife, but with God's help and through counseling (of a fellow pastor), we are able to continue in full-time ministry.[4]

The relationship of a minister's family to his work is explored

by the authors of *Ex-Pastors, Why Men Leave the Parish Ministry.*
Their research found, among many other things, that family
happiness is significant to the minister's success and happiness
in his role; that the minister's family life affects his own professional evaluation; and that the ministry is a strain even on strong
marriages.

One of their findings, which I think is particularly significant,
says, "There can be little doubt that the great majority of respondents look to their wives more than to anyone else to confirm the value of their work."[5]

Their statements confirm the significance of the minister's
family to the church and the church to the minister's family. The
family is an intricate part of a minister's job. The family significantly impacts the church job, and the church significantly impacts the family. This may not be the way it should be, and we
may be moving away from such a stance, but this is still an important factor to remember when making decisions affecting
ministers.

A series of articles written by Tommy D. Bledsoe, based on
his doctoral research, also validated my own informal probing
into the impact of forced termination. One woman he interviewed echoed my feelings when she said, "You cry a lot. You
begin to think you are alone in it. Nobody else cares or has ever
suffered like it in a church. You are disappointed in people."
Bledsoe points out that this woman is typical of others he
interviewed.[6]

Bledsoe says that forced termination may bring relief because
some closure is given to a major crisis. Remember, my first feeling was that of relief. However, he continues, the situation frequently has a negative impact on the family, the victim's main
source of help and comfort.

While many marriages and families are strengthened through
the trauma of forced termination, others show the strain of the

unanticipated and unwanted changes in life-style. Bledsoe reveals that for many there is the loss of self-esteem and esteem within the family, illnesses occur that range from minor to severe, and there are conflicts between family members.

He further notes one case, which he says is the exception rather than the norm, in which a pastor reported that had it not been for his family, he would have committed suicide.[7] Imagine the pressure on that pastor's wife as she tried to be supportive and caring for him while, at the same time, dealing with her own feelings!

Marriage relationships, according to Bledsoe, reflected the tensions, again ranging from mild to severe. Some marriages dissolved following the forced termination. He acknowledges that some of these marriages already may have been in trouble, but he believes that the forced termination crisis certainly did not help them.[8]

Bledsoe confirms stories I've heard and my experience concerning children. Their lives frequently are altered in a drastic way. They know, or sense if they are very young, that something is going on. They are hurt, and, in one documented case, respect for the father was lost. "Sometimes the minister's children suffer not only loss of valued friends, but academic and/or athletic opportunities due to timing of the ouster and ensuing necessity to transfer to another school."[9]

Bledsoe located people to interview for his research by searching a denominational newspaper in his state for ministers who resigned their churches without announcing future employment or people who announced vague employment plans. Also, attesting to the embarrassment, humiliation, and pain of forced termination, some of those who initially agreed to be interviewed canceled or failed to show for the interview.

Research conducted in 1980 by The Alban Institute, "A Study of Involuntary Terminations in Some Presbyterian, Episcopal, and United Church of Christ Congregations," indicates the reluctance of churches to talk openly about forced terminations. In fact, this reticence on the part of churches caused their entire study to be revamped.

Originally, the researchers planned to interview churches in the sponsoring denominations that had experienced termination. However, they were turned down 83 percent of the time by the churches, but very few ex-pastors turned them down.

The Alban Institute Study also found what our own conversations with victims of forced termination were telling us. Both the congregation and the clergy go through stages of grief similar to those described by Kubler-Ross in *On Death and Dying.*[10]

This study points out that the ending of a clergyperson's professional employment in the church is a particularly traumatic matter. Most persons enter this profession out of a high sense of calling and a perception that they have been set apart for this particular ministry. Failure in this calling not only means the loss of a job for which one has been prepared (as would be the case in any other profession), but it also probably carries the symbolic weight of disobedience to the calling that the minister believes came from God. Such dimensions add pain and misery beyond the brokenness experienced by other professions.[11]

This study also validates my belief that a minister's family and his career are integrally related.

One denomination does have statistics that prove Frank and I are not alone. The world's largest Protestant denomination, the Southern Baptist Convention, is acknowledging the growing seriousness of forced termination within its own ranks and is dealing with the problem in a variety of positive ways.

The Southern Baptist Convention, of which I am a part, is comprised of more than 37,000 autonomous churches, almost 14,800,000 members, more than 32,000 pastors, about 12,000 ministers of music, nearly 8,000 ministers of youth, 3,300 associate pastors, and 3,600 ministers of education. More than 22,000 students are currently enrolled in theological seminaries preparing for some form of ministry in the denomination.

Southern Baptists practice the congregational form of church government in which each church member has the right to participate in church government. This means that local churches are free to hire and dismiss staff members under that church's particular procedures. This autonomy also provides the arena in which forced terminations, justified and unjustified, can occur. No hierarchy evaluates and decides on the hiring and firing of personnel.

According to research conducted in 1988 by the Sunday School Board of the Southern Baptist Convention, 2,100 churches and ministers were affected by forced termination during an eighteen-month period. It further stated that 116 Southern Baptist churches and pastors are involved in a forced termination situation each month. Four years earlier their research indicated that number to be 88 per month.

The 1984 study also revealed that 91 percent of the respondents turned first to their wives for encouragement, counsel, and support when terminated.

This denomination is acknowledging the problem through formal resolutions and mandates to denominational agencies to engage in corrective and restorative actions. Opinions, comments, and suggestions, as well as tearful pleas, for help have been documented through books, numerous magazine and newspaper articles, and videotapes.

One of the most significant moves by this denomination has been the conducting of seminars for people who have been forced to terminate. An informal poll of men participating in these seminars revealed that two of the things they hoped to get from the seminars were "guidance in helping our mates" and "guidance in helping our children."

How I feel for all the wives represented in these statistics and stories! I know the burden that is on them. While the terminated person is turning to his wife, she has her own set of problems resulting from the termination. The burden on her is a heavy one. She needs help for herself and so that she may be a source of strength and comfort for her husband.

For me, a number of these statistics now have become real people with names and faces. I've talked with some of them and cried with them as I heard their stories that contain elements unique to them as well as situations similar to us all. So much of what they have said has mirrored my own experience. I have truly felt their pain. I've also heard things totally foreign to my own story—which further convinced me of our responsibility to help others. I know I am not alone.

All of this confirms my belief that many spouses need a book such as this, a book in which personal stories will reassure them that they are not alone, and a book that will offer them professional insights to aid their healing.

After all, we Christians believe in "bearing one another's burdens." We are in this together as long as any one of us suffers from forced termination.

It is probable that we will be forcefully separated
    from many people and things that are precious to us,
    and this separation will involve sorrow and pain.
    . . . .
It is important, then,
    whatever happens to us in our world,
    that our hope be focused firmly upon God
    and that our lives
    be involved in His eternal objectives.
                                —1 Peter 1, *Epistles/Now*

3
It's Like a Death
in the Family

My mother died—suddenly and accidentally—almost twenty years ago. Standing beside her grave at the cemetery following the funeral service, I watched all those cars passing by on the street. People were coming and going with their lives just as if this were another ordinary day.

The voice clamoring inside my head screamed at them, "Stop it! Don't you know my mother has just died? Don't you understand? How can you go on as if nothing has happened when my life has been turned upside down?"

I wanted the whole world to stop. Mine had.

Years later when forced termination abruptly halted the life we had known, I felt the same way. I couldn't believe that other people pursued their lives just as they always had when ours had been suddenly stopped for us. Again, I was forever changed by a loss that was out of my control.

If death has ever claimed a family member or someone very close to you, you know exactly what I am talking about. You too want to scream. You too wonder how everyone else can continue a daily routine as if nothing had changed.

Forced termination calls forth those same feelings. While there are differences between the loss of a parent and the loss of a church ministry job, the two are amazingly similar. The emotional, and sometimes physical, atmosphere surrounding forced termination is unbelievably similar to that felt when there is a death in the family.

Other women, wives of men in public jobs, feel it too, and they confirm our feelings concerning the significance and impact of the loss. Referring to the 1978 Massachusetts gubernatorial campaign in which her husband, then governor, lost the primary, Kitty Dukakis said the defeat "was like a public death" and the months afterward were a "period of mourning."[1]

Something is lost; gone and there is no way of getting it back. Life will never be the same again.

Our lives, we had thought, would always be spent working on a church staff as a minister of music. That was who we were. That was our calling. My husband, especially, could not see his life without a church staff job. He had trained for this role, and he planned to be a part of it for the rest of his life. Ministry through a church staff was everything.

In the wake of forced termination, sadness constantly enveloped me, and I couldn't quite shake it off. Remember how things are when you first awake in the morning, when for an instant everything is all right? Then reality invades your consciousness and you remember the forced termination. A day that briefly was a good day suddenly becomes one in which you are able to do only what life absolutely requires of you. You function at a minimum level. Sadness and sorrow cloud the day so that your full happiness cannot burst forth.

As they do when someone dies, most other people don't want to talk about it. Perhaps they think talking about it will make you hurt more. And, yet as the bereaved do with the death of a loved one, I wanted to talk. I needed to talk—just to talk and not necessarily to be given any answers or be told what I should think, do, or feel. Thank goodness I had a friend who could let me do that.

The most striking similarity between forced termination and

the death of a family member for me was that I mourned and grieved in much the same way for both experiences.

I discovered that husbands and wives probably will not grieve in the same way and at the same time. Frank and I did not. My feelings were from the very beginning those of a grieving person. However, it took longer for my husband to encounter and acknowledge the grief.

Practical concerns frequently consume one's energies following a death. Immediately following the termination, his attention and energies were focused on the very basic things of life— what we would use for money until he found a job. Would he find a job? How? When? Where? What kind?

He was too busy at this point to grieve. But, we found that, sooner or later, grief will catch up with you. Grief caught up with Frank after he had found a job in the secular world and when he realized he would not be going back into church work on a full-time basis.

When it hit, grief exploded from Frank with a mighty force. Although Frank is normally a mild-mannered person, he finally did blow, so to speak, and all of his anger came out. I have never seen him as angry as he was on one occasion, and that one time seemed to rid him of the physical intensity of his grief.

One difference between forced termination and the death of someone in the family is that, in the loss of this particular job, the "corpse" is still present. Daily I encountered people from the church. Even though many of them had not been aware of, much less party to, the forced termination, seeing them threw me into the "death" scene all over again.

And the church building went on standing just where it had for years! Nothing there changed! Just driving by it made me nauseous.

For a while, I returned to our church for worship services because our daughter wanted to attend. She had been a part of this church since her childhood, and most of her friends were there. However, as the services began each Sunday, I felt it physically. I could not continue there. I had to remove myself from those searing memories.

Those reminders hurt just as do those of my mother. To this day, going into a card shop at Mother's Day peels away the protective layers and exposes the pain. It takes so long and you don't really get over it. I felt it was so unfair that she had been taken. She hadn't done anything wrong. Why her?

These same questions grated on me again when Frank was terminated. Why him? He hadn't done anything wrong. I felt it was so unfair. But, one learns to deal with the loss. Each person has to work through her own grief in forced termination just as assuredly she does in the death of a person. Such tremendous loss does not have to mean your own death as well.

Others' Stories

"Mainly, I find in myself, a spirit of sadness or heaviness, as if there has been a death in the family," says Jackie. "It is very hard even yet, almost a year later, to have enthusiastic feelings over things that used to bring a lot of joy in church work."

"There is a hurt, and an empty space in our lives that will not be filled for a long time," explains Naomi. "For after all, we didn't lose a job. We lost a way of life."

"Consequently, we wrote a letter of resignation which, when read, came as a total surprise and shocked the congregation and choirs," says Mary. "A committee was formed to work out the final arrangements. We were 'retiring' early, so they even had a retirement banquet. The emotional upheaval of that event and our last Sunday simply cannot be described. It was as if someone who was very, very dear to us had died. Incredible sadness, even grieving took over. It was difficult! People phoned and wrote to us as it began to dawn on them what had actually happened. We appreciated their concern. It helped, but all they could say or do could not remove the devastating hurt.

"This is a grief experience, so expect a grief process to healing," continues Mary. "Our 'salvation' has been to find some other place of service. On Sunday mornings, I am the organist for chapel services at the Veterans Administration Medical Center, after which I go to play for a Presbyterian church. My husband goes with me and, even though he is not actually serving, it has helped him feel better as well.

"I know that time will heal, but I also know there will always be a scar as the memories will forever be with us, though I hope they fade. Fortunately, there are a multitude of wonderful memories also and from time to time we can review these as we view the many slides we took through the years of our church musical activities."

Margaret says, "First of all, I believe it is important to make a complete break. It does not help to heal when you see the people often, dwell on the circumstances or what is happening 'down at the church.' Remember, there is life after termination, and unemployment is not the worst thing that can happen to you."

"The pastor, who himself had just resigned, left for a week-long revival in another town, and he sent two men to my husband's office with the resignation request," relates Susan. "My husband considered taking it before the church, but knew this would hurt the body and might leave him in a worse position than he was in at the time. He wrote a gracious resignation and the minister of music read it to the congregation on Wednesday night. After the pastor returned from his revival, he never mentioned anything from the pulpit about my husband's leaving, nor has he spoken to us since. It is like we were never there.

"On Monday after the termination," continues Susan, "we went to eat lunch with a friend from the church. Another staff member came into the restaurant. He wouldn't even look at us or speak. It was like he was afraid to come close, afraid he would be next. We were amazed by this treatment. To this day, he has never mentioned what happened although he does make casual conversation with us when we meet.

"Our loss was not only of a 'job,' but a loss of ministry, church fellowship, financial support, self-esteem, and a good name, just to mention a few," concludes Susan.

"We visited our son's church one Sunday morning and the message was from Revelation 3:1-3," explains Annie. "As our son preached, I realized I have a name among friends, that I am alive, but down inside I am dead. God was saying to me 'wake up . . . I have not found your deeds completed . . . Remember therefore what you have received and heard; keep it and repent.' God still has a job for us to do and Psalm 51:12 is written in the margin of my Bible: 'Restore unto me the joy of Thy salvation, and sustain me with a willing spirit' (NASB).

"I began Bible studies after the initial shock wore off to prepare for the next assignment God has for us," she continues. "I want to be prepared for whatever God has for us to do whenever He is ready. And if He decides not to use us in this capacity again, at least it has helped me to grow. This is my real desire, yet when I think about them, as I write about them, Satan put the thought in my mind, 'That's a good approach. God ought to give you what you desire if you keep telling him things like that.' I then begin to doubt my motives for prayer and Bible study. Am I doing it for what I can get out of God or because I really want to serve Him?"

Continues Annie, "Our area has a 'building team' headed by

three couples who are Mission Service Corps Volunteers and made up of retired men. We have gone out with this group on four jobs, remodeling an old dorm into a chapel, remodeling two small churches, and constructing a new building for a mission. These are times of work, fellowship, sharing, and Bible study. We have received encouragement through the prayers and fellowship of new friends as well as longtime friends and a sense that we have accomplished something for the Lord's work."

Dan's Observations

Forced termination is indeed very much like a death in the family. Something very dear and vital has been taken away with no options available to the victim.

Other people don't want to discuss it. They will talk all around it, but never approach it directly. Or they will not give you an opportunity to talk out your grief.

If people do talk, they frequently offer meaningless platitudes. No real help is offered nor does any real communication take place.

As in the death of a family member, the lives of the survivors must be reoriented. Changes must be made to compensate for the loss. Finances must be scrutinized. Frequently, new methods of providing financial income must be found and adjustments in your style of living must be made. Often, you must relocate to another house or another city. Other family members may have their own particular needs resulting from this termination/death, and you are compelled to offer them help.

Conversely, there are also significant differences between forced termination and a death in the family.

Society, and especially the Christian community, has a well-defined process that supports a family when someone has died. A ceremony, in which the deceased is acknowledged and many times praised, marks the time and place of the one lost. "Casserole Christians" take over and a steady stream of support flows to the survivors. Many practical details, such as preparing food for the family, assisting with funeral arrangements, cleaning house, and running errands are done by these supportive Christians. Frequently financial aid is offered. When a family member dies, the survivors are not blamed but are offered support and encouragement.

However, when the loss is a highly valued position in the religious community, things are not quite the same. No casseroles and no stream of support expressing belief in you and your future come your way. Or if they do, they are few and far between.

The old cliché, "The Christian army is the only army that shoots its wounded," has far too much relevance during these times. Instead of rallying around the terminated, many people move away from them. In a forced termination, many other ministers do treat you differently. Susan's summation from her own experience was correct. Many ministers distance themselves for fear it could happen to them.

The token appreciation, if there is any at all, from the church is frequently awkward and painful. It is not a ceremony in which hope is offered, and it is never quite comparable to the investment you have made. As Mary related to us, this "appreciation" often appears to be something totally other than what it is.

When a family member dies, the finality of that is marked by the physical absence of the deceased. And this contributes to a new beginning for the survivors. In forced termination, as Myra has pointed out, that "corpse" is still visible in encounters in church and around town.

Losing a loved one to death is an extremely significant loss, a loss whose importance we do not want to depreciate. But, a forced termination may, in some ways, have more impact on the individual.

In forced termination, there is loss based on years of investment, and it is not an unimportant loss. It is the loss of an ideal. We are talking about the very essence of a person's life.

Ministers do not go about their careers as do many people. Their ministry totally encompasses the entire personality. It infiltrates the ego and the personality development, even in the early stages, as a person brings together his or her Christian faith and commitment to a career. Christian faith and career become inseparable in the minds of the minister and the family.

So when you talk about the loss of a church position, you are not just talking about a minor element in one's personality. You are talking about a major loss. You are talking about a major restructuring of the personality, separating your church work from your faith in God, and separating your own career—with such heavy identification—from your own relationship to God.

You have, indeed, been disconnected, terminated from a role often perceived greater than that of a job, a marriage, or any other significant relationship. It is a greater grief because it strikes at the core of your spiritual self. You have been officially rejected by those in whom you have invested spiritually . . . and financially. For instance, how does it feel to know you have invested 10 percent of your income in an institution that is telling you it no longer needs you? In my office, ministers and their spouses have shared with me exactly how this feels.

In many ways, the grief experienced in forced termination defies comparison. But, your reaction to the loss of this position is very definitely a grief experience. Your grief is very real; it is natural; and it is necessary. The intensity with which you will grieve is in direct proportion to the degree of your investment in what was lost.

You can expect to grieve and realize that your grieving is a part of the journey toward healing. Most people are aware of the stages of grief designated by Dr. Elisabeth Kubler-Ross in her research with dying people. In her book, *On Death and Dying*, she delineates these stages as denial and isolation, anger, bargaining, depression, and acceptance.

While it's really all a matter of words, I have modified these stages of grief somewhat for my own use: I see the stages of grief as shock or numbing, denial or disbelief, negotiation with God, and, finally, the resolutions stage in which you pick up and go on with life.

Most people are shocked when forced to terminate. Many of them had no indication that termination was in the offing. They didn't see it coming. Others, while there may have been conflict in the church, are totally unaware that such a thing could happen in a church.

These people start trying to make sense of what has happened to them, and it can't be done. Denial is the stage at which you keep acting as if the termination hasn't happened. You continue with life as usual (or as usual as possible) and refuse to believe termination has happened. In denial, your mind refuses to accept reality. Your mind will do that when your entire belief system is based on your need for that job. Your beliefs say life without your job would be void. Your mind cannot conceive of life without it.

So, you negotiate with God. If God will intervene; if God will make it all go away; if something can be done to avoid the embarrassment, the humiliation—then you will sacrificially give your life in service to God.

Resolution comes in time when you've exhausted negotiation. You accept that it will not go away. It has happened, and you must invest your energy in the future and not waste it on the past.

The healing has now begun. There are ways you can cultivate the healing process.

Allow yourself time to grieve. Remember that I said grieving is natural and is the only road to recovery. Just as a baby cannot walk until he crawls, you cannot really begin to feel good and be ready to move on until you acknowledge your grief and deal with it.

Grief is not alien to the human experience. It is as natural as the developmental stages of life. Grief is a built-in condition and is experienced at all levels of life—in the loss of a home through a fire, in the loss of a pet, a significant person, or a job.

God has blessed us with grief as a natural process for handling loss. The way in which you have handled loss prior to termination ought to be a good indicator of how you will deal with loss here. Some people process it pretty well, and others get stuck in stages of the grief process.

The point at which you get stuck, it is believed, is the point from which, sooner or later, you will have to pick up and move on. You may be stuck there for years. I've counseled people who remained stuck for eight to ten years in the denial or negotiation phase.

Many are surprised to find the grief process tied into the calendar. As the anniversary of their loss comes around every year, they become seriously depressed. You may find yourself depressed before you are even aware of why the depression is upon you.

Some people who have every right to grieve and who should be going through a legitimate grief process will not allow themselves to do so because a voice from their past prohibits it. Someone in their past has told them such things as: "Don't feel sorry for yourself. There are plenty of other people in the world who have it worse than you do. You should be ashamed spending so much time thinking of yourself."

Such logic is no help at all. Many people mistake a genuine sense of loss with self-pity. Instead, it is a feeling of depression that is a natural part of the grief process. It is irrelevant to someone who is going through grief to know that someone else has it worse. It is not irrelevant, however, to know that someone else has been through it, cares about you, and will support you through it.

Human beings need to grieve. It is all right to grieve. So allow yourself some time. Acknowledge what is happening to you and don't be too hard on yourself.

However, don't stay in your grief. The grief process has value for a while, but not forever. It is helpful to "do something" to help the grief process along. Also, because one area of your life has been controlled by someone other than yourself, you will feel better about yourself by taking charge.

The following activity is especially helpful in the earlier stages of grief. Give yourself ten minutes (Set the timer!) to think of all the bad that you can. Dream up the most terrible things that can happen because of this forced termination. Write these down. At the end of the time, stop abruptly. But it is important that you also use the full ten minutes. If you run out of the worst possible things that can happen before your time expires, create some! Fantasize.

Now, do the same things with all the good things that could possibly result from the forced termination. Do this for ten minutes, and write them down.

Condense from those ten minutes of positive thinking one sentence that might read something like this: "It is OK to be out of control for the moment. I can always allow people to do what they must do, knowing that ultimately God and I will make something good come from this."

In addition to this statement, practice imagery for ten minutes. Picture yourself—and this has to be in the form of a scene—experiencing something positive, something that is healthy that has come from the forced termination. You could see yourself in a new role, a new career, or with you and your husband happily working together in the future.

By thoroughly imagining the *worst*, you have already taken care of it and can tell yourself when the worst scenario arises, "Oh well, I've already covered that, so I won't waste time thinking about it again."

By imagining the best, you've set in motion conditions your brain will tend to seek out, even unconsciously. Ideas will begin to rise to the conscious surface, and with these ideas you will begin to build the future. Only hours before you could not conceive of any other role in life. Now, you've opened up the future. There's hope. And depression cannot coexist with hope.

I continually tell our staff that problems are only the absence of ideas. When you start creating the "best case scenario," you've unlocked the box that has imprisoned your mind and limited your opportunities.

Another action that will help you through the grief process is to find someone with whom you can talk. Myra noted how important this was to her. This could be a friend with whom you can be totally open and free so that you can describe your real, true feelings. Talk to someone who can let you have the feelings that go with the grief process. It needs to be someone who loves you and accepts you without being judgmental, someone with whom you feel secure.

The person with whom you need to talk may be a trained counselor who will listen and who can also give you some specific help. Both you and your spouse may want to use this time to undergo testing that measures your strengths as individuals, your personality traits and characteristics that are most likely to offer you a clear picture of what you ought to be doing with the rest of your lives. Remember that God can use a professional counselor, just as He may be using this book now in your hands. In another chapter we will go into more detail about finding support through both of these methods. But, talking with someone is important to your well-being.

Another important facet of successfully negotiating the journey through grief is to take care of yourself physically. As we know and have had illustrated for us already, a crisis tends to affect our physical beings as well as other parts of our lives.

Physical exercise is extremely important. My own experience with exercise has made a believer out of me, and I recommend it to all my clients who are going through difficult times.

Exercise does two things. It purges the system by burning up the adrenaline that accompanies many of the feelings you are having during this time. Also, it makes you drink much-needed water for the purging of your system, which tends to keep the body functioning well.

Psychologically, exercise is a distraction. It enables a person to do something that is helping. Knowing that one is doing something to help brings about a calm, a peace, and a resolution in the mind. Also, when exercise is done outside, being exposed to nature seems to remind us that nature is bigger than we are, that in the midst of troubled times, trees still grow, rivers still flow, and birds still sing.

Exercise does not have to be complicated or expensive. It can be simple. However, the method of exercise chosen should be within your physical limitations and under your own doctor's recommendations for your particular needs.

A very important thing you can do is to find projects in which you can participate, and pour yourself into them. Find something you can do and complete. Then stand back, look at it, and feel good about yourself.

You read the story of Annie, who said she began Bible studies in preparation for the next task God had for her. She was doing something worthwhile, as well as gaining knowledge and understanding.

Another assignment I have for you is to find things that you can do for other people. For years, I've been making this particular assignment to my clients who were experiencing grief or major transitions in life. I give them assignments that have to do with giving of themselves to others less fortunate. Something very healthy happens when the focus of your attention is taken off yourself and you are able to give of yourself. You feel needed, and you also begin to get life in perspective. You realize that what is happening to you is not the worst (although it is certainly not the best!) that could have happened.

Annie told us about remodeling and building churches with a group of volunteers. Not only did she and her husband do something very worthwhile, they found fellowship and comfort with other loving people. Mary related to us that it was helpful to her when she again began playing the piano for church services. We have already referred to the book written by former President and Mrs. Carter. It is full of examples of how they became involved in volunteer work, and it offers suggestions (complete with the names and addresses of the agencies) for things others may do.

Your denomination and the religious, medical, and social services groups in your city are but a few of the places that can use, and indeed need, volunteer help. While you may not feel like involving yourself in this manner, frequently becoming involved anyway changes those feelings.

Finally, I recommend that you memorize and recite the Serenity Prayer. Most of you are familiar with it already. I use it regularly with clients who have lost all sense of control over their lives. I have found this to be the most profound statement in the mental health world that relates to the healing process.

The Serenity Prayer
Lord, grant me the serenity to accept the things I cannot change, the courage to change the things I can, and the wisdom to know the difference.

We are not to play God in his life,
    determining his goals and indicating his actions,
    but the role of comrade, friend, and brother,
    seeking together, ever learning from each other,
    what is God's best for us individually and mutually.
    . . . .
At the same time, we do need to be aware that
    there will be troublemakers amongst us who,
    though they claim the Christ name and insist
    they are living by His grace and guidance,
    are the very instigators of division and dissension.
We are to continue to love them —
    and prayerfully strive to draw them into the peace
    and joy of a right relationship with God.
                   —Romans 16, *Epistles/Now*

4
Keep a Grip on Reality

When a person is devastated by something such as forced termination one's mind can play tricks, so to speak. Mine did! You begin to think strange thoughts that may have no basis in reality.

I recall Dan telling me at the time that one irrational thought feeds on another, and they go on and on until you build an entire belief system on irrational thoughts. Because of this the body chemistry changes, and you make yourself sick.

Is that ever true! As I've said, I began to think that everyone in town knew what had happened to us and that everyone in town was discussing it. I felt conspicuous, self-conscious. I would look at people and wonder what they knew about us and what they were saying to other people. In reality, not even everyone in the church knew what happened. But, embarrassment was among that host of feelings I had during this time. Because some people did not appreciate and want Frank, I inferred that a lot of other people thought the same—or they were at least wondering if we were good enough. Talk about rejection!

I felt the church was saying, "We don't need you." This led to wondering if God needed me.

The aloneness I talked about earlier entered into this rapid growth of irrational thoughts. I felt alone and all my negative thoughts intensified rather than eradicated this aloneness.

The other prominent thought, which I now know to be irrational, was that I had lost my identity and my husband had lost his identity. I thought that we had lost all that we had worked so hard for all these years. I came to realize that if we were working for eternal things, they are not lost. The results are stored up; we may never even see them, but they are not lost.

Others' Stories

"I came from an emotionally abusive home," explains Justine. "I was an abused child and grew up knowing rejection from my mother. I never was able to live up to my mother's expectations. I still don't know what they are. But my mother was mentally, emotionally, and sexually abusive. My father, who was nonsupportive, had his own 'escape mechanisms,' even to the point of attempting suicide. My 'family' was my church. That's where all my 'pats on the back' came from.

"I learned early in life that being sweet, looking pretty, and being good were what brought me acceptance from the world. So, to state matters simply, when my husband was fired from the church, my 'family' (the church) kicked me out—total rejection. Not only did I not have a real family, but my substitute family had told me that they did not love me, no matter how sweet, how kind, or how hard I worked. I was devastated!"

"Why are second staff members expected to stand up for the pastor and back him in every way, even when they know the pastor is wrong, but a pastor doesn't feel it necessary to stand up for the other staff members?" questions Annie.

"I had to rethink and revise how I think about God and how He allows terrible things to happen, and yet remains unchangeable in His love, promises of security and seen or unseen support," says Jackie.

"God did not fail us, people did," concludes Mary.

"As a way of coping, I began to logically think about and remember the successes of the past . . . how God had called us and how He has led us and blessed us," says Susan. "Through this rational thinking I could tell myself God has not left us. He is still here and we will make it through the valley."

Dan's Observations

All of us are security-minded people. We want to know that our needs will be cared for, that our future is assured. We buy health insurance, even burial insurance, in order to be sure we will have resources when sickness and death occur. We put money into retirement funds so we will be able to live securely in our old age. Security is important to all of us, and we do innumerable things to foster that feeling.

However, there is no security in the life of a minister. There is an illusion that ministers have security because God calls them. We also assume that everybody in the church is going to adhere to the voice of God in the same manner. That is not necessarily the way it happens.

The church, the institution that employs you, is not run as are other institutions, for the most part. There is no union. In the congregational form of church government, there is no hierarchy of management or authority. No one is up there to protect you. Each church has its own method, sometimes a confusing maze, by which it selects staff ministers. You cannot predict what will happen at the next church or the next time by using your previous experiences.

A church can make a decision, especially if the decision is placed in the hands of a few influential people, that is totally unethical and make it seem ethical because it comes from the church. In the attempt to resolve problems, a church may discharge somebody by saying, "God said we should do it." Who can challenge that?

Churches ought to operate more like a business in that they operate with written guidelines. Ministers should have an opportunity to face accusers and tell their story. The United States court system does that, but churches don't.

So your security is placed in a very unusual and interesting institution.

As you begin to consider the possibility of being terminated, even before it becomes a conscious process, the unconscious belief is that if this church should terminate us, then our future is bleak.

In the first place, there is a stigma attached to a minister who is asked to leave. That is a stigma essentially and specifically identified with the religious and church community. After all, if God called you here, what is the message? Is God rescinding His call, or is God punishing you? Does God no longer see you as a valuable, worthwhile person?

In addition to the spiritual dimension is the broad, American view of success. The male population, and increasingly the female population, is faced with a tremendous amount of pressure to succeed. This is true of ministers. Yet ministers are the only professionals I know who are expected to succeed without appearing to be ambitious. The success factor is no less a powerful one in the life of a minister than it is in any other career. So, you have the spiritual dimension and the broader view of the success image with which to contend.

Your peers and fellow professionals will have questions. If forced termination has not happened to them, they don't understand how such things can happen. Since the church is of God and the church is composed of many, many minds working together, there's the assumption that they—the church—must be right. The assumption is that if the majority voted to terminate this person, the church must be right. So, there's a big question mark on the one terminated. What did he do?

When you are being considered by another church, there's a stigma attached if you have left a church without somewhere else to go. So if a church is considering you, this raises a question in their minds. They don't know about you and what happened, and there is no good process for them to find out the truth.

Now, when the whole basis for your employment, professional, and financial security are threatened with possible or actual termination, you experience fear. Fear is an emotional response to a perceived threat.

With this emotional response of fear, the mind begins to do what psychologist Albert Ellis termed, "awfulizing." Ellis is the designer of RET, Rational Emotive Therapy, which says the rational mind should control the emotions. When a person is "awfulizing," she says such things as: "If I do this, so and so won't like me. If so and so doesn't like me, then she will influence others not to like me. If others don't like me, they will also reject my husband. Since they reject us, he will lose his job. I will be embarrassed. I will be a failure. We will not be able to get another church. If we are not able to get another church, we will be rejected by other ministers and the denomination, and we will have no future in the church."

"Awfulizing" continues to get more and more irrational with things such as: "My husband isn't trained to do anything else. He will not be able to get another job. He will not be able to support the family. My family will then see me as a failure. Our friends and our extended family will see me as a failure."

This goes on and on until a person sees herself without resources with the creditors beating on the door. She may even envision bread lines and soup kitchens. More realistically, she will recall the "no good" uncle who was a "bum," the one of whom everyone was ashamed. And she will begin to identify with him.

Thinking can get so irrational at this point that a person sees no reason to live. I'm not saying that she is in fact, suicidal, but she begins thinking at this point that life would not be worth living. I've had clients tell me: "Dr. McGee, I would never take my life, but I don't want to live anymore. I wish an accident would take my life."

This is the time for serious intervention. Do not permit yourself to live in this kind of depression. Unfortunately, it may get worse, and you could lose the capacity to think rationally.

Understanding how emotions are affected by thoughts is enormously important for depressed people. The human brain seems to produce more negative than positive thoughts. This negative orientation is a means of survival, a defense mechanism. Thoughts definitely impact, influence, and lead to emotions. Once your thoughts have affected your emotions, your behavior is influenced as well, creating a cycle of thoughts, feelings, and actions.

Where the cycle starts is unimportant. It is important that people understand that thoughts (cognitive domain) which begin to deteriorate into irrational thoughts will determine a person's emotional state (affective domain) and consequently their actions (behavioral domain). So it's important to stop that process before it worsens. At this point you need to visualize, or create a picture in your mind, of a future that utilizes your skills and that utilizes the personal and collective resources that you as a family have, no matter what the outcome of the church's decision.

The only way that your brain's negative tendency can take hold and dominate you is if deep down at some unconscious level you already believe you are *not OK*. If you deeply believe you are OK, that you are worthy, that you are valuable, and you are confident of that worth and value, the negative stigma attached to forced termination doesn't stand a chance with you. When those thoughts come along, your mind may have a tendency to think them, but they cannot take root and grow because you find these thoughts inconsistent with your basic philosophy in life.

In summary, you say to yourself: A church is made up of fallible people just like me. If any portion of that church makes a decision to terminate our role, it has absolutely nothing to do with our value in God's sight. We have the necessary resources as a family to redirect our lives and move on with our future.

By the time a minister's family reaches a crisis such as forced termination, each family member has established a cognitive belief system—a philosophy of life, beliefs about life and oneself, and one's relationship to the world. The behaviors resulting from this belief system have become habitual. Much like the knee jerk response, it is difficult to say why you do some things. You just do them. They are automatic and require no immediate, conscious thought on your part.

This cognitive behavioral system, composed of beliefs and actions acted on over time, are necessary for normal daily activities and are the foundations for decision making and actions that may involve major changes in life.

The Creator equipped us with a marvelous capacity to store thoughts and use them without having to think consciously about every detail as they arise. It is believed that conscious thoughts take much more energy. Thus, we would be exhausted if we had to rethink everything every time a related issue arose. So, the unconscious mind serves as a reservoir of stored beliefs, or conclusions about life, out of which we think and act daily. These conclusions about life may have caused a few problems here and there, but not until a major life crisis such as forced termination did they produce emotional problems, some of which can be serious.

Let me give you an example of how our basic belief system can awfulize until we are seriously ill. Look at how the thought processes affect our fictitious minister's wife, Jane.

1. Jane grew up believing that a female's role in life was one of supporter, encourager, enabler of some male in her future. During her childhood and adolescence, this was modeled by her parents and reinforced by her environment.

2. As a Christian, Jane also grew up believing God had a plan for her life and that her relationship to God was determined by her following that plan. Jane comes, over time, to interpret her choice of John as her husband and her role as a minister's wife as that plan.

3. Jane, along with John, believes God's approval is tied to their carrying out God's plan for their lives. In other words, John must succeed in his role as a minister. Jane must support and enable this success or they have failed in God's eyes. Specifically, Jane believes that if John fails, she has failed.

4. In order for this couple to succeed in life, church members must respond favorably to his leadership and her role. Thus, if they are to please God, they are to please the people.

These four beliefs are unconscious beliefs. They have been so ingrained that Jane and John act out of them without even thinking. When John reports to Jane about the conflict between him and a specific church member, why does Jane immediately become physically ill? She, literally, becomes sick to her stomach. Her pulse rate soars, her blood pressure rises, she breaks out in a cold sweat. Over days, she may even begin to lose weight, become edgy, and experience long periods of silence.

The answer to this question is that in her view her relationship to God and her role in God's world are threatened. Her entire identity as a minister's wife and supporter is at stake. Her success in life is threatened.

Now, here are Jane's conscious thoughts that arise from her unconscious beliefs.

1. John and I have failed.

2. I have failed John. That is, John isn't happy because of me. I haven't made him happy. If I had done a better job, this would have never happened.

3. I have failed God.

4. We will be rejected by church members and friends.

5. John will not be able to find another position. He will have to leave the ministry.

6. His training is wasted.

7. My sacrifices are for nothing.

8. We will be rejected by other ministers and families.

9. We will be viewed as failures by everyone.

10. My parents will not understand, and I will be a failure in their sight.

11. We will be destroyed financially and be dependent on others.

At this point, Jane is seeing images, which is another part of the cognitive domain, another thing that emerges from the belief system. Images include scenes or pictures in her mind of people in the past whom she was taught were or learned to interpret as losers. Depending on Jane's unconscious beliefs about herself, her self-esteem, this process can get much worse. It can lead to depression.

Under the category of self-blame, here are examples of what Jane can tell herself.

1. I'm not good enough for John. He could do better without me.

2. I'm a loser. Not even God accepts me.

Under the category of blaming others, Jane might tell herself:

1. I hate those people. It's their fault. I hate church people.

They're to blame. They are all alike.

2. I hate God for doing this to us. God promised to take care of us if we did it His way. God has forsaken us.

This is awfulizing. Thoughts grow increasingly worse, bringing about a state of depression. The trouble with depression is that it no longer creates only negative thoughts, it creates a biochemical imbalance in the brain which lowers psychic energy and contributes to a negative attitude about life in general.

For example, Jane's negative thoughts might lead her to think, *Not only are church people bad, but all people are out to get you. You can't trust anyone.*

She could also begin to think, *Not only has John lost this position, but he'll probably be fired anywhere he works. Why go on trying?*

Earlier, I implied that the thought processes, conscious or unconscious, are the basis for the behaviors people choose to act out. Over time, when behaviors continue to result from thought process (belief systems), the knee jerk, or automatic, reaction is established.

For example, Jane no longer thinks consciously about avoiding church members, which is a behavior, since they all represent a threat to her identity and life, which is a belief. Every time the phone rings, she avoids answering it without even thinking. Her avoidance pattern has become automatic, but it is based on the belief that other people are a threat to her.

It is vitally important that Jane recognize and deal with this conscious chain of thoughts that deteriorates into withdrawal and serious depression.

The solution to breaking this chain of awfulizing can be found in the next chapter as I suggest exercises to help you deal with stress.

While most of you will not find yourselves in an extreme situation emotionally, some people may suffer severely from the effects of forced termination. I am including here the warning signs of mental illness, which have been compiled by American Psychiatric Association president, Paul Fink, M.D. He advocates informing the public about these warning signs so that early diagnosis and treatment are possible. If you or your husband see yourself in this list, please seek help.

The Ten Warning Signs of Mental Illness

1. Marked personality change
2. Inability to cope with problems and daily activities
3. Strange or grandiose ideas
4. Excessive anxieties
5. Prolonged depression or apathy
6. Marked changes in eating or sleeping patterns
7. Thinking or talking about suicide
8. Extreme highs or lows
9. Abuse of alcohol or drugs
10. Excessive anger, hostility, or violent behavior

The tragedies and conflicts of this life
    will discourage us,
    but they can in no way change God's attitudes
    or stifle His love for us.
Failures and defeats may trip us up,
    but such do not affect our relationship to God.
Our boat will rock; the earth will tremble.
Revolutions will shake up governments and institutions.
Our traditions may be nullified;
    our convictions threatened.
Every temporal security may crumble.
But God's love and reconciling grace are forever,
    and He will never let us go.
If our allegiance is to God and our faith is fixed on Him,
    the very atrocities that seek to destroy us
    become the means
    by which He carries out His will
    in us and through us.
                            —Romans 8, *Epistles/Now*

5
This Is Stress

Sleepless nights, churning stomach, frequent crying jags, dark clouds of depression, waves of nausea, listlessness, bewilderment, irritability—these and a host of other confusing feelings have become your unwelcome, but constant, companions.

A thought, a song, a memory, or just dealing with the problems of daily existence—any number of things can generate a bolt of lightning from the storm cloud that seems to be always hanging over your head these days.

Participating in church, a valued and necessary part of one's life, becomes difficult, if not impossible. If you are able to go, you may feel sick and cry the whole time you're there. A passing encounter with someone from the church knots your stomach into a tight ball, and haunts the remainder of your day.

You probably don't need me or anyone else to enlighten you at this point. You know well that you are suffering from stress. Indeed, you probably have experienced enough termination-induced stress to write your own book!

Making a job change of any type rates near the top on life's stress charts. You and I know being forced to leave a church job carries with it emotional and spiritual baggage not found in other types of work. Therefore, we can safely assume an even greater stress level.

Escape seems a wonderful way to cope with this stress. If only we could just leave and not have to deal with anything. That's what I wanted to do, but the way I chose to do that was not healthy.

As I've already told you, my own skills for handling stress had never been completely adequate. Stress-related problems were already present, making my physical problems more severe when forced termination dumped even more stress on me. In talking with other women, I've found that some of them also experienced stress-related physical problems, even while enjoying the ministry they felt called to do.

Getting physically well was crucial for me. As I've said, the blessing was that I had to quit taking tranquilizers in order to have surgery. While recuperating from that surgery, I had a time free from any kind of pressure. Being free of the prescribed drugs and having to stay still and quiet so my body could heal from surgery created an atmosphere in which I could begin dealing with the problems forced termination created for me. Many days I sat perfectly still in a chair and just let myself be.

Although we will discuss it more fully in another chapter, let me say here that seeking professional counseling was essential for me in managing stress. I needed to acquire specific skills for coping.

That's when I called my brother for help. Of course, therapists are not permitted to treat members of their own families, so he could not provide the actual counseling for me. But, even if these restrictions had not prevented him from being my counselor, our personal relationship would have. I remember him saying, "I can't treat you Myra, because all I would do is sit and cry with you."

He did use his professional training and experience to help me, but, as he said, he had sense enough to know he couldn't be my therapist. My brother introduced me to a Christian psychologist in his clinic and continually supported me by being available when I needed a brother.

Counseling enabled me to know how to deal with the stress effectively. It gave me specific tools so that I could "do something" instead of being overwhelmed. I learned to cope by making a conscious decision each day about how I would react when I encountered something that reminded me of the forced termination, which for me was a guaranteed stressful situation. I was changing my coping skills, and eventually these skills became, for the most part, a natural part of myself.

Notice I have not said I have no more stress. I do. I expect stressful situations of various kinds to be with me always. What I now have is a way to handle the stress so that it doesn't control my life. I can, in fact, move forward and live more fully.

The stories other women told me revealed that my feelings and responses were not unusual, even though we may have reacted to stress in different ways. I have learned from these women, empathize with them, and feel a bond to them. Perhaps you will also.

Others' Stories

"I think the Lord had strengthened me through the heartbreaking experiences of dealing with a rebellious teenage son and the loss of my father when I had to search the Scriptures and allow my faith to grow to survive," says Dianne.

"Pain, which I never knew existed, so overwhelmed me through the months and years we were dealing with our son that I thought we would never know happiness again. Now, our son is progressing positively, and we realize that time does take care of many things. Throughout this time and through the illness and demise of my father, my husband was much stronger than I. But I grew through the grace of the Lord and realized the sufficiency of Him. I feel that day by day He was teaching me through trial after trial that He was there.

"So when the next trauma struck, that of forced termination," Dianne continues, "I was the stronger one this time because through my weakness and pain previously, I knew that I would become stronger or completely destroyed, and the Lord was merciful."

"It does not help to heal when you see the people often, dwell on the circumstances or what is happening 'down at the church.' We stayed in the city, spending the first couple of months visiting other churches in the area, exposing our family to other denominations as well as other Baptist fellowships," explains Margaret. "This gave us time to heal somewhat.

"We cut our expenses by deleting unnecessary items from our budget. Of course, our savings were depleted and our daughter in college took a year off to work and save for future expenses. Most ministerial families are used to pinching pennies so this was not too hard a task.

"Our main objective is to get through the forced termination experience without becoming bitter.

"Where we go from here is not quite certain, but I am very comfortable where we are and will be ready to face the next challenge a little wiser and stronger."

"My borderline high blood pressure problem for which I was taking medication was aggravated by the stress of forced termination," says Mary.

"I cried a lot, often unexpectedly, which has been embarrassing, but helpful, I'm sure," she notes. "From time to time I've been asked to sing a solo or lead the music for a Sunday School event or other special occasion. Suddenly, a wall as real as concrete rises between me and that situation. I simply cannot do it.

Just thinking about it arouses all the original upsetting emotions."

"I can find no explanation—at least one which I can understand—for well-meaning people who continually ask why we don't come back to the church services since we still live in the city and have kept our membership at that church.

"The worship services were our 'chief' responsibility, so attending services only reopens the wounds and scrapes the emotions raw again," says Mary.

"The first time I entered the sanctuary again was on a weekday afternoon. We wanted to show our out-of-town friends where we had invested our lives. I was standing with them in the balcony, looking toward the choir-pulpit area where my husband was busily arranging the lighting as he had done so many times to show the beauty of the vast 2,200-seat auditorium. Suddenly I felt physically ill and excused myself. As soon as I was outside, the nausea subsided."

"At the time of the forced resignation, I was still recovering from gall bladder surgery, which I'd had two months earlier," she explains. "After the forced termination, it was difficult to sleep at night. I spent several days crying and was very depressed. I was numb. I literally had to force myself off the sleeping pills prescribed by my doctor."

"I suppose I have read three hundred books in the last ten months," says Annie. Many of them are for spiritual help and guidance, but I've also read many novels, mysteries, historical and gothic romances, and Westerns. These help me relax and take my mind off 'my problems,' as I call our situation. These books have shown me that other people have problems, many far more traumatic than mine. It's an old cliche but still very true: We can always look around and see someone with more troubles than our own."

"I became so physically ill over my husband's forced termination that I could not eat. I filled many long, dark hours of the night by writing letters to God in which I told Him my fears and concerns, prayed for my husband, thanked Him for my husband's influence and effectiveness as a father, and thanked God for the close relationship my husband and I have. These late-night epistles also included my own request for the strength to endure.

Dear God,
     "It seems I continue to have trouble sleeping. My heart hurts, my stomach is in knots and my head seems so confused.
     "Lord, you know and I know that I love you very much. I want to serve you every day, but I'm having a hard time. I don't understand why all of this is happening. I feel very rejected and hurt. The person I love the most next to you has been done very wrong by Christian people. That makes my heart ache.
     "Father, I want to depend on you but right now I'm not sure where you are. Please help my lack of faith during this very difficult time in my life.
     "I need to be the best wife and mother that I can be during this time. I feel like a failure at everything. Strength for these days has been hard to find.
     "Lord, I don't feel that hard times aren't going to come our way, but I need to know you remember me and are going through this with me. I can't seem to grasp hold of a handle to help me through these days.
     "My prayer tonight is for strength and courage to handle each day, for wisdom for Mark in making the right decisions for our family.
     "Thank You for keeping mine and Mark's relationship strong during this. I love you for that!
                                                            "I love you,
                                                            "Lisa"

Dan's Observations

Stress! Hardly a word is more abused and less understood than stress. Since 1978, when I sat in awe as the late Dr. Hans Selye, the undisputed grandfather of stress research, demonstrated the effects of stress on laboratory mice, I have pursued the implications of stress on our daily lives.

I've listened to Myer Friedman, M.D., the famous "Type A" discoverer, tell us how heart disease and the personality are linked together. From Menningers to Johns Hopkins to Harvard, I've sought out the experts to learn from them what they know about stress. The primary focus of my studies and research has been the effects of treatment on stress-prone individuals.

At the time of this writing, my "ABC's of Stress" program has been the exclusive group therapy stress management program in seven private psychiatric hospitals. Each issue of "The Metro-McGee Report: The Stress Digest" presents to the public the best of what we are learning about stress.

What have I learned about this misunderstood word? That *stress* is *not* a four-letter word! That even though it has brought us heart disease, headaches, digestive problems, back pain, respiratory and skin diseases (and countless others), it has also helped us do such things as bring children into the world and prepare them for adulthood. Stress, by means of blood, sweat, and tears has brought us freedom as a nation. It has given us education, marriages, and career accomplishments.

For me, studying and writing about stress has produced a great deal of stress. I sometimes feel like the client of mine who said, "Dr. McGee, I'm so used to being tense that when I'm calm, it makes me nervous!"

Seriously, not all stress is bad. Dr. Selye helped me understand the difference in healthy stress, or eustress; and unhealthy stress, or distress. I've learned that what is distressful to some of us is fun to others. I've learned that the secret lies in the match of mediating, or coping skills, with the appropriate environment. We can improve these skills by understanding and improving our thought processes through the regular exercise of healthy thinking. I've learned that certain "automatic" responses to stressors in our lives were not always automatic. We can unlearn and retrain ourselves to think and act in new ways repeatedly until these responses become "automatic."

I've learned that just as God equipped our bodies with a miraculous alarm system, He also provided a built-in calming system that with practice we can learn to call on request. And, I've learned that this miraculous body is continuously giving us signals through nerves and muscles, biochemically through blood and hormones, and even through the distribution of body temperature.

I've discovered personally and through countless hours with stressed hospital patients that we can learn to pick up these signals and act to reduce stress before its damaging effects can be felt in the body.

These are the stress lessons I shared with Myra while she continued in therapy. Nowhere have I encountered a more determined pupil than Myra Marshall. She listened even when the message was painful. Myra crossed a line, turned a corner, one day as if to say, "I have nothing to lose. I am dying, and I want to live. I choose life!"

Two powerful childhood lessons were learned from our parents by each of the five McGee kids. From our father we learned *survival*. To Ed McGee, you may be down, but never out! You were never truly without resources. You just dig deeper to find them! Giving up has never been an option. Myra, Edwyna, Dan, Esther, and Johnny—each has known pain, grief, and struggle, but none has known surrender.

From our mother came an incredible sense of humor. What an important balance to the survival ethic. We laughed ourselves through conditions that ought to have drowned us. The message was clear. "Don't take yourself so seriously that you lose the capacity to laugh." Her sudden death resulting from a horse-riding accident shook our family to its core. But even then I recalled her humorous wish for an epitaph to be written over her grave: "I told you I was sick."

As I studied the work of Norman Cousins in his wonderful book *Anatomy of Illness from the Viewpoint of a Patient*, I recalled the lessons in humor taught us by Hazel McGee. The evidence is still building regarding the role of humor in stress management.

Stress Management

Whenever faced with a stressful situation, you have three options, each beginning with the word *change*. You can:
1. Change environments
2. Change *the* environment
3. Change yourself

Change Environments

Changing environments means picking up and leaving the scene of the crime, so to speak. Most people who are forced to terminate have no choice about changing environments. You must leave the church, if not the city. However, some effects of stress may follow even though you go to another city.

There are two levels of environments. First is the church itself. Second is the city or geographical area surrounding the church. If the church is located in a small town in which social life revolves around the church, then the two environments really can be viewed as one. However, if the terminating church is one of many churches in a large city, then the environments are distinctly separate. But, remaining in the city may still trigger negative thoughts and feelings as you pass members' houses and encounter members in shopping areas.

Myra and Frank decided to remain in the same town, and she kept her job in a place where many people would know about the church situation. In fact, members of "The" church also worked in the same building with Myra. Other forced termination victims may leave the church, but likewise stay in the same town. Some have no choice but to stay until work and a new home can be found. Although removed from the primary source of stress, they will encounter people, places, and situations that can cause one continual period of stress.

Surely no family, even if they stay in the same town, would continue attending the church that had terminated them. I have heard of some who had to return to the terminating church weekly to pick up their severance pay. If at all possible, don't allow yourself to be put under that kind of stress.

Changing, or leaving, your environment should not be viewed as running away. There is no virtue in staying in a place or situation that is so overwhelming to you. Why stay in the environment and constantly expose yourself to all the pain associated with it?

On the other hand, while you choose to leave that congregation, you may not be able to leave the city or geographical area. We've heard of many forced termination victims who had purchased homes in the town where their churches were located, and since they were near retirement age, they could not afford to move. Some lived near adult children and did not want to leave. With every member of the family comes an increase in the number of variables with which you have to deal. Frank and

Myra considered the needs of their teenage daughter, as well as their own, when they decided to stay in the city where she had spent most of her life. Home ownership, proximity of children and other family may add up so that you ought to stay in the city where you are.

Some people never consider leaving the area, and for others that is the first thing they do consider. Escape, whether it's good or bad, is relative to the other options open to you. People who are prone to escape for some reason don't usually try the second option, which is to change the environment. But, because the act of changing environments, or relocating, itself carries a certain amount of stress with it, a person should try to change *the* environment or change herself before choosing the option of leaving the area altogether.

Change *the* Environment

Changing the environment means negotiating with it, influencing it, manipulating it, doing whatever you have to do to get a better match between you and the environment. It means altering the environment to meet your particular coping skills.

Negotiating with the terminating church itself in order to change the environment would be direct confrontation. It could be the terminated person and spouse meeting with the persons responsible for making the decisions, presenting their case, and challenging the decision. That would be an attempt to change the events, decisions, and stressors in the environment in order to minimize the stress.

This confrontation can be done in a written document, itemizing your view and your perspective of the situation. Written documents are, in my opinion, an excellent way to say what you really intend to say without getting sidetracked and having to

react and say something you don't want to say. Also, there's a
record of it so that years later, if the subject comes up again,
everything is in writing. This would be an attempt to negotiate
with the church environment.

The wife of a terminated minister might be able to negotiate
with her environment by going to her circle of friends and finding or creating a support group. She may choose to be very
open and honest, indicating her need for understanding and
support at this time.

If the terminated family chooses to stay in the area, even in a
large city, they must determine the extent to which they will
avoid reminders of the old church or directly counter these reminders with a new attitude. The new outlook while remaining
in the geographical area brings us to our third option.

Change Yourself

This third option involves the choice most often the most
challenging of the three. This means (1) to improve your coping skills, and (2) to improve your perception of the environment. That is, look more rationally at your own abilities and
capacities and develop thought skills with which to interact with
an environment that may or may not change.

Probably the most valuable of these coping skills would be
the capacity to block things out when faced with a series of dis-
appointing events resulting from termination. Periodically give
yourself a day when you are not going to worry about the
forced termination and all the problems associated with it. You
are going to enjoy the day. You are not going to be consumed
by this problem. The capacity to choose what you are going to
think about is a coping skill and is normally developed in the
process of growing up. Sometimes choosing not to think about
a painful situation can be difficult. Take a small step at first.

Read a good book; enjoy a movie; call a friend. Each choice makes the next time easier.

The ability to not take an action or event personally is a coping skill. By personally, I mean to deduct from the event that (*a*) I'm bad, and (*b*) what they did was intended to harm me personally. Using this coping skill, you stand back and try to get in the other person's shoes and look at what kind of decision making might have led to this decision or these events. The ability to objectify is a coping skill.

Again, we are talking about a mismatch (between coping skills and demands of the environment) when a person needs to be objective, but tends to take things personally. Here you have an environment where a lot of decisions are being made for you. In order to survive that, you need to be able to look objectively at the event, detach yourself as if you were not really the victim. Some people have developed this skill over years of experience. If it doesn't exist as you encounter the termination experience, it is difficult to create on demand. At this point, your best avenue for gaining objectivity will be in therapy with a trained professional until you are strong enough to develop your own objectivity.

Another coping skill is focusing on something else by completely losing yourself in some cause, some ministry, or some endeavor that is very fulfilling. Recall the woman who told us how she and her husband used this method in order to cope. They joined a group of retirees in their denomination who remodeled and built churches. They found a place of service where they were needed and benefited from the fellowship of people who were committed to a common task. Also, she began Bible studies to prepare herself for whatever God had in her future.

A part of improving your coping skills is exercising your faith, by saying, "This is bigger than I am. I cannot handle it, but God can. Lord, you will see me through."

The forced termination experience is a good time to reevaluate yourself and make some improvements. Just as physical pain can serve to motivate a person to action, so psychological pain can serve as the foundation for emotional and spiritual growth.

Because you have been forced to leave your church against your will, you and your mate probably have been consumed with questions of what went wrong. Where did you fail? Could you have done something differently to prevent this? In some cases those people who called for your departure may have also told you where and how they think you failed. A person who hears criticism should consider it, even if the criticism flows from a terrible source. The church may have had some valid reasons for terminating you. Now is a time to be honest with yourself. However, the church may not have had such reasons, and you should not try to punish yourself.

Never assume that the termination is all your fault. Neither should you assume it is all the fault of the other party. However, people do tend to view the rightness and wrongness of such an event in one of these ways. Either of these can block real growth.

Do you think "they are right and you are wrong"? If that's true, then you are devastated. You probably feel as if you are a big zero, nothing. If you make that assessment, then your self-esteem must be rebuilt.

The second problem comes in viewing the situation as "they are wrong and I'm right." If that is your conclusion, then there is no room for error or evaluation. This viewpoint is as bad as the other.

A healthier perspective is that everybody experiences everything in life from their own viewpoint. The rightness and wrongness of things is based on a set of beliefs and conclusions we have about life when we enter that conflict, problem, or situation. Everybody is as they are for a reason. Most people are not just mean for the sake of being mean, nor are they thoughtless because they enjoy being that way.

To gain objectivity, consider all the things of which you are being accused. Ask yourself which of these have any reality and what you can do to improve? Also ask yourself these questions: What are the areas where I may be seeing "bugger bears?" Where am I accused but know I am not guilty? An objective counselor or therapist can help at this point, and we will talk about how to select a counselor in a later chapter. Mustering up that objectivity is extremely difficult when your whole security is out on a limb.

Now, with those considerations about improving yourself highlighted, let's talk about changing yourself by changing your coping skills so that you can handle stress more effectively.

You possess a lifetime of coping patterns that enable you to manage or hinder you from managing this latest adversity. Every unexpected disappointment you have experienced has prepared you for dealing with your forced termination, whether you are aware of it or not.

For example, recall Dianne who said earlier in this chapter that the illness and death of her father and also the years of dealing with a rebellious teenager prepared her for managing the crisis of forced termination.

Think about your situation. A great deal of your preparation for this crisis came in early childhood as you observed your parents coping with adversity. How did they handle it? What messages were left indelibly recorded in your mind?

What kind of crises did you encounter as an adolescent? Were you allowed to face things and experience a sense of confidence when you worked your way through a traumatic or challenging situation? The brain retains these experiences in the form of verbal statements that you hear repeatedly as you confront your current crisis.

Your brain also retains images, pictures of these crisis events. You can recall that moment years ago when you received the "bad news." Practice it for a moment. What sounds, verbal messages, have been recorded in your brain from that event? What pictures do you see as you think about that horrifying experience? What conclusions did you draw from that experience that still govern your life today?

All these fall into the cognitive, or thought, domain. They are the thoughts, beliefs, images that have become a foundational part of your life. So integral are they that they affect your perception of life and guide your reactions to it. My research, as well as that of many others, has demonstrated the impact the cognitive domain, or the thought process, has on one's feelings and actions.

At this point we can help you change your ability to handle stress. You can learn new ways of stress management.

Three approaches to the treatment of stress are widely used: biofeedback, relaxation/training, and cognitive behavioral stress management. Each of these has been thoroughly researched and proven effective for certain individuals under specific conditions.

A few years ago, I devised a simple, effective method in order for people to grasp any kind of stressful situation. My method falls under the cognitive behavioral stress management approach. It has been used successfully in very large corporations, federal agencies, and psychiatric hospitals.

McGee's ABC's of Stress, in its simplest form, recognizes what I call the three functional domains: (*a*) the *affective* or feeling domain; (*b*) the *behavioral* or actions domain; and (*c*) the *cognitive* or thought domain (See diagram, p. 97).

In learning to manage stress, we must intervene at A, B, or C. My program addresses C, the cognitive domain, because C most

ABC's of Stress
Three Functional Domains

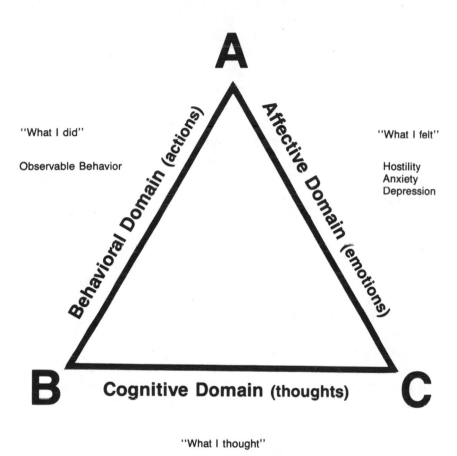

A

"What I did"

Observable Behavior

Behavioral Domain (actions)

Affective Domain (emotions)

"What I felt"

Hostility
Anxiety
Depression

B **Cognitive Domain (thoughts)** C

"What I thought"

Conscious Thoughts
Nonconscious Thoughts
Imagery

dramatically affects A and B. Our thoughts directly influence our feelings and behavior. I try to teach people to identify the irrational thoughts (unhealthy conclusions) that lead to negative, destructive emotions. If we can change the way we view or think about our environment, we can alter our emotional stress responses (feelings).

Within the cognitive domain are three categories of thought: conscious thoughts, imagery or the pictures you hold in your mind, and nonconscious (unconscious) thoughts, which are beliefs or attitudes you hold but don't consciously think about. Please note that here I have chosen the word *nonconscious* in preference to the commonly used words *unconscious* or *subconscious*. Nonconscious thoughts are those that exist in the mind and are available for recall, but are not in the immediate awareness.

Following the steps in the Stress Assessment Chart (a sample has been completed for you at the end of this chapter), you can learn to recognize your negative or stressful emotions, behaviors, and thoughts, and you can learn to replace them with the positive emotions, behaviors, and thoughts.

Use the blank chart provided for you at the end of this chapter for your own personal assessment. Write down the stimulus or the triggering mechanism that caused you stress. Then, following the chart, write down the emotions you felt when the stimulus occurred (step A). Make sure these emotions are true feelings such as hostility, anxiety, depression. Write down the behaviors you acted out, the conscious thoughts you had, and the nonconscious or irrational beliefs. In the last step, record the negative images your mind envisioned.

On the right side of the chart, write down the emotions you would like to feel when the stimulus occurs again. This part can be fun because you are dealing with the positive side of things. In the same vein, write down the behaviors, thoughts, beliefs, and images you would like to have. Fill in each of these blanks in light of what you would like to have happen when the stimulus occurs again.

Now, I have an assignment for you, something you can do that will help you handle your stress.

1. After completing your assessment chart, return to shaded area.

2. Select one conscious thought and circle it. Select one belief and circle it. Select one image and circle it.

3. Set aside five minutes three times each day for two weeks. Use two minutes to rehearse the new thought, two minutes to rehearse the new belief, and one minute to rehearse the new image.

4. Select two actions that will express the thoughts, beliefs, and images recorded in the above shaded area and act these out at appropriate times over the next two weeks.

Your new self-statement (based on beliefs you'd like to hold) might be something similar to this: "I am an adequate person. I am a competent person, and I will perform adequately."

One woman with whom we talked said she coped by remembering and thinking logically about the successes of the past. "I thought about how God called us, how He has led us and blessed us. Through this rational thinking, I could tell myself God has not left us. He is still here, and we will make it through the valley."

This person was reminding herself that she and her husband had been adequate people who handled their lives successfully in the past and that God had been with them in the past. By doing this, she was making her own self-statement that these things were still true in their present lives. She was reassuring herself of their own adequacy and God's continued presence, no matter what decisions others made for them.

Practice saying your own new thoughts, belief, and image

three times a day, for two weeks. Consciously select and act out the behaviors that are consistent with your new thought, belief, and image. A new healthy behavior might be to call a friend who will listen to you and accept your feelings. Ask her for her prayers and support. Another new behavior would be to speak confidently about your future.

By doing this you are reinforcing in your own mind that you are competent enough to do the necessary things in your life. You are rehearsing healthy thoughts and acting on them consistently in your daily life.

My prescription sounds simple, but it works and can be applied to all stressful situations. If you think healthy and act healthy, one day you discover those negative emotions are becoming the positive emotions you have desired. And you are learning to handle your stress in a much healthier manner.

While on the subject of stress, I want to say a word of warning about a dangerous method of stress management. This greatly used and abused form of treatment is prescription drugs. Drugs have played a strategic role in our society in the treatment and prevention of disease. However, in almost every case medication should be a means of achieving some form of stability while nonmedical treatment is undertaken.

As is always the case when an effective solution is found for the problem, the solution becomes a part of the problem. Frequently doctors will prescribe drugs in order to give the patient relief from physical pain. Such was the case when Myra's body began deteriorating under the continuing burden of emotional stress.

The doctor says, "This will help for a little while, but you have to learn better ways of managing the stress." For emphasis, I repeat that while there are truly some good and healthy uses of medication, with very few exceptions medication should be seen only as a brief, temporary method of stabilization to prepare the patient for nonmedical methods of stress management.

No one wants the psychological pain associated with stress, such as hostility, anxiety, or depression. But, before you too quickly medicate those symptoms, consider what you are doing. You may be masking the problem. You may be chemically tricking the body into ignoring nature's own method of alerting you. Anxiety serves a purpose. It is an alarm system. If medicated, it may never challenge the real problem at all.

Also, one can become dependent on drugs, even those given by a physician. My company devotes hundreds of hours each year to hospitalized adolescents and adults who are chemically addicted. These are not the "down and outs" of our society, but are mostly upper- to middle-class Americans who can afford private hospitalization. They range from small business owners to corporate managers to professionals to Ph.D.'s to physicians and their family members. So, don't think it couldn't happen to you.

Prescription addiction has become such a problem because it is accessible to middle-class Americans, and it is impossible for the medical profession and the Food and Drug Administration to control. Unfortunately, it has been seen by both patients and physicians as a legitimate method for managing stress. I do not agree. I believe the risks far outweigh the possible positive outcome. Safer methods of stress management are available.

If you believe you can handle the stress in your life, you can. The simple exercise we have just detailed gives you a concrete, safe way to enable you to do that.

Name (Your Name)

Date (Date of Assessment)

McGEE'S ABC STRESS ASSESSMENT

Stimulus (a recent event which resulted in stress for you): Saw Mrs. "X" at the supermarket. (Her husband was chairman of the committee responsible for the decision to ask my husband to resign.)

	WHEN STIMULUS OCCURRED:	WHEN STIMULUS OCCURS AGAIN:
STEP A	Emotions I felt — Anger, depression	Emotions I'd like to feel — Calm, self-confident
STEP B	Behaviors I acted out — Avoidance	Behaviors I'd like to act out — to converse with my normal schedule, speaking confidently to those I encounter.
STEP C	Conscious thoughts I had — How will I have to endure this kind of rejection and humiliation someday. Nonconscious thoughts/beliefs I had 1.) She probably agrees with the decision 2.) Everyone else probably does also 3.) No one cares about us 4.) We are all alone in this 5.) I failed somehow. Images — I see a picture of our family isolated and alone with no normal	Conscious thoughts I'd like to have — I hope Mrs. "X" can understand someday what I feel. (1.) Mrs. "X" may or may not agree with the decision 2.) likely many others would reject the decision if they knew the circumstances 3.) they do have to go make a decision 4.) Support is available from actions (and God) when I need it 5.) My Boss (God) will continue to do so) Beliefs I'd like to hold — the next I can do and will Images I'd like in mind — I see a picture of our family smiling, arm in arm.

ASSIGNMENT

1. After completing above, return to shaded area.

2. Select one conscious thought and circle it. Select one belief and circle it. Select one image and circle it.

3. Set aside five minutes three times each day for two weeks. Use the first two minutes to practice recreating the stimulus (top of page) using the new conscious thought circled above. Use the next two minutes to rehearse the new belief circled above. Use the final one minute to rehearse the new image circled above.

4. Select two actions which will express the thoughts, beliefs and images recorded in the above shaded area and act these out at appropriate times over the next two weeks.

Name _____

Date _____

McGEE'S ABC STRESS ASSESSMENT

Stimulus (a recent event which resulted in stress for you): _____

	WHEN STIMULUS OCCURRED:	WHEN STIMULUS OCCURS AGAIN:
STEP A	Emotions I felt _____	Emotions I'd like to feel _____
STEP B	Behaviors I acted out _____	Behaviors I'd like to act out _____
STEP C	Conscious thoughts I had _____	Conscious thoughts I'd like to have _____
	Nonconscious thoughts/beliefs I had _____	Beliefs I'd like to hold _____
	Images _____	Images I'd like in mind _____

ASSIGNMENT

1. After completing above, return to shaded area.

2. Select one conscious thought and circle it. Select one belief and circle it. Select one image and circle it.

3. Set aside five minutes three times each day for two weeks. Use the first two minutes to practice recreating the stimulus (top of page) using the new conscious thought circled above. Use the next two minutes to rehearse the new belief circled above. Use the final one minute to rehearse the new image circled above.

4. Select two actions which will express the thoughts, beliefs and images recorded in the above shaded area and act these out at appropriate times over the next two weeks.

We can and must agree on the prime requirement
   of every Christian,
   that we learn how to love and care for one another.
                    —Romans 14, *Epistles/Now*

6
The "For Better or Worse" Faces Testing

Seeing anyone mistreat my husband has never been easy. You know what I mean, I'm sure. So far, I've not met a wife who felt her husband deserved to be terminated or deserved the manner in which his forced termination was conducted.

You see, I know my husband. I know his commitments, his intentions, his desires—all of the things that may be unknown or misunderstood by people in the church. I've always wanted everybody to like him. In fact, I was hurt and upset if everyone didn't like him. I wanted to say to all those people, "If you only knew him the way I know him."

Even with being so convinced of my husband's fine qualities, a thin line of doubt crept in, just briefly, during my worst hours of depression. (Those irrational thoughts!) I had always thought he was so wonderful, but was he weak for just resigning and not "standing up" to the church? Another fleeting thought was one that I had never had in my marriage. I thought, *This is his problem, not mine!* I was embarrassed. I wanted to run.

But, those were only brief doubts. We were supportive of each other during the forced termination, especially after I was able to function.

The solidity of our marriage was our main asset in surviving this forced termination crisis. Frank has often said, "I've doubted many things in my life, but never my marriage."

Looking back on our decision to marry and knowing it was the right one supplied that foundational strength for us. We were committed to each other and to our marriage. United and together, we were "fighting the enemy"; not each other.

Other crises, of varying degrees of seriousness, which we had encountered as individuals and as a couple prepared us for dealing with this one. However, although we were secure in our marriage, we differed in our reaction to the forced termination. In so very many ways, Frank, by his example, was a model for me as we moved through this termination.

Frank is a very healthy person and has difficulty knowing how to relate to someone who is sick. So, while I was on so much medication, he was away most of the time looking for a job and then traveling for the job he accepted.

Frank is also independent and resourceful. He moves ahead with determination. During this time, staying busy was important to Frank. He says that the realities of the forced termination gripped him a couple of times, but he just "put it off." He told himself that he didn't do anything wrong, and he was determined to show "them" he could survive without their job. He did not want their pity.

Falling apart, Frank has always contended, was not an option for him. Frank believes deciding how you will act or react is a decision you can make. Some things he would not do. He would not go back to the church. (The first time he went back was for our daughter's wedding several years later.). He would not discuss the church in any negative way. He would not turn down supplying in the pulpit for anyone who asked him. And he would not join a church where he was just a member and not able to work as a staff member.

Frank is a doer, an action person. He doesn't particularly want to talk things out. He says if he can do something, he will do it. But, he is not a listener who can empathize. He doesn't want to sit around and talk about it. If he does, when he gets through, he says he wishes he had said nothing.

On the other hand, my tendency is to talk things over. Talking is my way of working out problems, looking at options, and looking for reasons. Many times, I've had to say to Frank, "I don't want you to fix things or to do anything. I just want you to listen." Dan says that most men have this need to fix things.

We probably did not talk as much as we should have. I felt Frank was so fragile. He had always been my rock. But then, I felt that if I leaned on him or was possessive, he would have backed away. The fear that he might have a heart attack or go completely bonkers haunted me.

The only time our relationship was really strained was when both of us hit bottom at the same time. Our family has always prayed together about things that concerned us. Even now, we ask our adult children to pray about certain matters at specific times so that we all are praying together even though we are in distant locations. However, there were times following the forced termination when Frank and I could not pray together. At times when the wound was as open as if it were new, we would be too emotional to pray together. Both of us would end up in tears.

I remember walking into the room and telling Frank, "Today I can't handle your being weak. I'm sorry. Today, I just don't have any strength." And there were times when he would say essentially the same thing to me.

Frank did get a job, related to music, but not related to the church. He traveled a great deal, and his office was in our home. He missed having an office at the church to which he could go every morning, and he missed the interaction with the staff people. And though he moved ahead with determination, trying to enjoy and to become involved in his new work, there were many days when I dearly wished I could swap places with him so he could go into an office.

We also tried to protect each other, which I learned is not uncommon for couples going through a crisis. As we began to heal, we became aware of or encountered other couples who have been forced to terminate a church staff position. Frank, particularly, has done specific things to be supportive and helpful to men in this situation. Often we have taken the couples out to dinner just so they can get a break from the battle and so they can talk with someone who really does understand.

Most people I've talked to—and this was also our experience—were not willing to say things to each other that they would reveal to someone else. During these dinners, the husband would say something about his feelings or personal struggles to us. The wife would respond with "I didn't know he felt that way." And then the opposite would be true when she shared something very personal that he knew nothing about. They would never have said those things without a third party being there to pull it from them.

It was at one of these dinners that I heard Frank say, "I will hurt every day the rest of my life. There will never be a day I don't hurt." He hadn't told me that! He thought I was too fragile to handle it.

I firmly believe couples need to talk with other people with whom they can identify. Many feelings will come out when talking with others that will help you to understand your mate.

For me, our relationship has improved as we have worked through this crisis. While I have always loved my husband, I like the one I see now more and more. As he has moved through the process, Frank has changed for the better. He used to expect me to be at the church for everything. Now, he's much more aware of my needs and commitments outside of church. He is much more easygoing these days. In the early days, he was always "go, go, go and push, push, push." Now he is soft, warm, and listens well.

Frank has extended this understanding to others as well as to me. He identifies with church members' lives and commitments more easily today. I've heard him say he wishes all staff people could be laypeople at some time in order to better understand the other side.

Dan has said that Frank is now a more well-rounded, interesting person who sees the world from a much broader perspective. While he is still committed to the church, his life is not so totally wrapped up in it.

Others' Stories

"My greatest frustration," says Annie, "is seeing my husband suffer through this termination. He has always been a very active person. We are financially unable to travel, which we both love to do. He can't fish. He had just sold his small boat, planning to buy a larger one, when he was terminated. There is nothing he can do in a small town such as the one where we live—a town where people outside the church knew what happened even before people inside the church knew. Physically I can see a change in him because he feels bad so much of the time—nothing in particular, just feels lousy. And there is nothing I can do to help him except pray for him and encourage him not to lose faith.

Annie continues, "The church he is in as interim music director just wants him to lead the singing and have choir rehearsal if they feel like coming for it. He gets so frustrated when he sees the need for education in the churches and they aren't interested in doing anything, even when someone is available to help them with no charge to them (except work on their part), especially when they complain they don't know how to be a Sunday

School director or teacher, they don't know how to lead the singing in their church, etc. But when he offers to help them in any way, they just back off and won't make a commitment to learn."

"The most degrading thing was to have to pick up my husband's check each week, to see the people at the bank, and so forth," remembers Lucille. "What I actually experienced was relief. I had to be strong to make decisions and listen. We were shocked, hurt, and angry. My husband is by nature a very strong person. However, he almost crashed completely. We went through the process of trying to find another church, and he still hasn't given up on that completely. But, we knew he had to find a job, which he did. There are days when he enjoys it, but most days he leaves home depressed because he doesn't have a church. He is the one who has been affected, physically, mentally, and spiritually. He is angry with God and man. The children and I have been able to go on. In fact, he accuses us, saying we do not want him to get a church. In a way, that is true. I had physical problems, mainly my stomach, when I was in church."

"The relationship I have with my husband is one of the things that has helped me through this time," says Lisa. "I feel like such a failure at everything, and I've prayed about the need to be the best wife and mother during this time. Strength is hard to find. I thank God for keeping my relationship with my husband strong during this time."

"Throughout our married life, my husband has been a source of strength and encouragement to me, and now I find the roles reversed as he faces disappointment time after time in either not hearing from an employment application or finding the job to be totally unsatisfactory," says Naomi. "I feel the Lord has made me stronger, and I find that I am more totally committed to my prayer and devotional life as I seek to find answers for our lives."

"It has taken several months to overcome some of the demeaning statements made by the pastor to my husband," says Susan. "At one confrontation, the pastor told my husband he didn't think he (my husband) was 'called' and that my husband had no commitment. That cuts deep and is a wound that takes a while to heal."

"My husband was lynched that night, and there was nothing I could do," says Beth.

"Because I knew that my husband had done a good job, because I knew this (forced termination) did not come from our people, and because my husband was so devastated, this time I had to help my husband," says Dianne.

"My husband and I leaned on each other heavily," says Susan, "just being together, talking things out, helped."

Dan's Observations

During my years as a minister of education, my wife Sandra and I had to consider each employment opportunity based on the quality of the health facilities in the area. As our hosts would show us around town, they seemed a little distressed at our request to see the local hospital. During a particularly difficult time when my health problems put me in one of these hospitals, Sandra came to my room with a large poster that showed two dogs leaning on each other, looking woefully at the viewer. The caption said, "It's you and me against the world, baby."

That is the message your husband needs from you right now. He needs to know you are with him, right beside him. The major function of the family today is survival, much as it was in

prehistoric days. The adversary may be of a different nature
than in those early days, but the role of the family in survival
today is very much the same. Evidence shows that people in
families live longer, have fewer illnesses, suffer less mental
stress. So the family is supposed to be a resource in times of
trouble.

Corporations and institutions generally do not love you, per
se. They cannot hug you. They cannot tell you they love you.
Individuals within the institution can, but the institutions themselves cannot. We must have a family, we must have the support
of a close group that believes in us, that does not lose faith in us
when things like this happen. You are your husband's primary
source of support right now.

Two of the most potent things you can say to your husband
are, "I believe in you," and "You have the resources."

As a therapist, I have to be supportive of my clients, even if I
am not supportive of their behavior. I use these supportive
statements regularly, and they are extremely powerful.

Your support is paramount. Your husband does not need you
to join the criticism of those who may be critical of him at this
time. Rather, he needs you to believe in him, to constantly reinforce him through your supportive role by telling him, "No
matter what comes or goes, what actions are taken, no matter
what happens, I am here. I'm going to love you. We are going
to see this through together." With that kind of support, a
bonding takes place, the kind of bonding that should take place
during a crisis.

In dysfunctional families, this is not the case. An unhealthy
family self-destructs when faced with a crisis. This could be absolutely devastating to a minister also going through forced termination. It is natural and predictable, although I don't know
that it is healthy, that one's self-esteem is going to suffer in a
time like this.

Almost all marriages have something to build on, however. Find the strengths in your marriage and celebrate them. You need them now.

The length of time you spend in crisis is important. Much like high tech equipment at the breaking point, your coping skills also have limits. A couple stuck in a crisis will eventually see coping skills break down. In anger and frustration they may very well turn on each other, blaming each other. For assistance in a prolonged crisis you may need a counselor with sufficient experience to recognize danger signs.

Do not linger in the wilderness beyond the value it has to offer you. If you stay too long, the negatives will drag you down. You need to get out. As limbo goes, not too much good can be said about it.

What are some of the things you can do to be supportive of your husband and help him through this crisis?

Recognize that the forced termination may have little or nothing to do with the strengths or weaknesses of the one terminated. Churches are systemic organizations. They may be ordained of God, but they are governed and administered by human beings. Anyone who believes that the majority is always right hasn't read two pages of history.

You may be terminated based on conditions beyond your control. I regularly consult with corporations based solely and legitimately on profit motive who are compelled to make survival decisions resulting in termination of employees from the chief executive officer down to the parking lot security officer. These decisions frequently have nothing to do with competence or incompetence, and, consequently, it's OK to grieve the loss. But you must separate their decision from your own value as a person.

Remember that everything is a matter of perspective. Right or wrong may be difficult to determine. Ministers often have bad habits. My favorite is crediting God for whatever the minister thinks is right. Remember that deifying my choices no more makes them God's choices than calling a toadstool a mushroom makes it edible.

Allow other human beings the option of being right or wrong regarding the termination. Let them have their perspective. It could be a good decision for the church and for you. Not all events result in winners or losers. Sometimes both win, or seem to win; sometimes both lose or appear to lose for the moment. You may feel you are in the darkest night right now, but a future, brighter than you could ever imagine, may be waiting for you.

When I made the decision to leave local church work and go into the field of professional counseling, no one would hire me. I had numerous opportunities to continue in the religious education field but nothing in my newly chosen field. Within a few years, psychologists and psychiatrists who earlier would never have hired me were working for me.

What appeared to me to be loss turned out to be the best direction for me, my family, and my career. It may be that forced termination is the door of opportunity for you and your family. Our society is winner conscious. But, remember we worship heroes only until we find their humanness. Then we tend to destroy our heroes. Let others think what they need to think about you and yours when forced termination happens. Thoughts are temporal and are easily influenced by next year's events.

Believe that you are blessed, special, and chosen. Frankly, I cannot explain why this works, only how. My late grandmother wrote a marvelous novel on the life of Joseph. Although it was never published, my grandmother's novel made a profound impression on me. Her book helped reinforce a belief that I've held since childhood, a belief that I was blessed, that God had something special for me to do.

My parents had dedicated me to God before my birth, and they frequently told me so. In my early adult years, I grew to resent that because I felt I had no choice in the matter. But, as time passed, I believe God enabled me to see what it meant to believe, in the Old Testament sense of the word, that I was truly blessed.

My grandmother's torn and tattered manuscript sent me back again to the story of Joseph. No matter what terrible actions were taken against him, he suffered temporarily and then flourished. I believe two things contributed to his unimaginable success. He believed from childhood that he was blessed. And, he took adversity as an opportunity to succeed.

Parenthetically, there is another lesson from Joseph for forced termination victims. He had a sense of humor. I think he laughed inside while watching his brothers who had betrayed him, now in Egypt trying to figure out what was going on. So, never lose your humor. If you think you have, go find it. It's not lost; there's still time to retrieve it.

Why do great comedians focus on misfortune for comedy? That's where most of the humor is. The unsinkable Norman Cousins has taught the world that just as depression inhibits the body's immune system, laughter seems to strengthen it.

Finally, remember that ultimately failure is not failure if it leads to success. Besides, I'd rather fail while trying than to fail while wondering if I would have failed while trying.

What is failure anyway but finding a better way to succeed? Remember to do something. Try something. Don't wait for God to send something your way. Go out and explore the options, believing God has something special for you and knowing God wants you to find it. There may be something He wants to teach you in this process. Moses went *to* the burning bush in the wilderness. God could have burned a bush on Pharaoh's porch. I believe Moses was looking for a bush regardless of his fear.

I once saw a photo cartoon of a big ape scratching his head. The caption read, "Sometimes I sits and thinks and sometimes I just sits." Don't just sit.

In the early days of psychology, we seemed to be bent on defining mental health in terms of what it was not. Studies focused on depression, anxiety disorders, and the psychopathology of the disturbed patient. Then came Abraham Maslow and his attention given to healthy, self-actualized people, followed by healthy family studies by Jerry Lewis of Dallas and later Nick Stinnett, John DeFrain, and associates of the University of Nebraska.

After fifteen years of outpatient and inpatient psychotherapy with thousands of people, I decided to make a list of things missing among psychologically impaired individuals and necessary in recovery of mental health. I identified nine things happy people seem to have in common. You and your husband may want to look for these in your own lives.

1. Happy people have imagination. They seem to generate ideas. They like to create. On one of my trips to the White House, I was asked to wait in an office in the Executive Office Building before I would be escorted into a press conference where the president would address the nation. As I sat in this beautiful historic office with high ceilings and a fireplace, I began to wonder who had sat in this office and what ideas might have been conceived in this very room—ideas that are today a part of our daily lives. As I looked around that gracious old room, I realized that every branch of our government was once nothing but an idea in somebody's head. I reached across the desk on which speeches were written that day for the president to give to the world, picked up a sheet of White House stationery, and wrote the words, "The future is in the mind of to-

day." I still have that note to remind me that imagination is God's gift for our future.

2. Happy people believe in themselves, that they are no less than a creation of God, that they are unique and an unrepeatable miracle . . . and therefore of great worth. People of worth do not put themselves down. They acknowledge imperfections and fallibility while seeing themselves valuable. Happy people allow themselves to be en route. They see life, not as a destination, but a process, a journey. They are able to accept themselves (as God does) without losing sight of the goal. Researchers have found that individuals who believe in themselves, who believe they have the resources to deal with crises, in fact, tend to cope better with crises.

3. Happy people give themselves to something outside of themselves. Depression studies have shown that people involved in a good cause fare better than those who withdraw and turn inward. One reason for this has to do with breaking the downward chain of negative thoughts by focusing on something positive and productive. Such a person begins to feel needed and senses his or her value to the cause. Another reason for their happiness has to do with a support system that often is produced by people working together toward a common goal.

4. Happy people prioritize. Insecurity is often expressed in our inability to say no to some opportunities. That person who says yes to everything and everyone without regard to her own energies, skills, and interest will soon feel trapped and angry at all those she is trying to help. Accepting the fact that in this real world we all operate with "givens," limitations imposed on us by virtue of our humanness, this decision alone gives us freedom otherwise unavailable to us. Only in exercising our right to say no are we really free to say yes to opportunities. Every no to someone is a yes to someone else. All opportunities available to us, all choices we must make are not equal in value. They must

be weighed in the light of *our* goals, or we will be overwhelmed, drowning in a sea of good options.

5. Happy people deal with pain and sorrow but seek out the good that can be learned from it. Some life events do carry the potential of devastation for us. But why is it that the same event is experienced differently by two people? One may never recover from loss while another seems to grow, to build on that loss. It is important to acknowledge that while we would never choose tragedy, we must choose our response to it. And that response itself is more important than the tragedy itself. The event itself cannot make you a bitter and lonely person, only your response (the conclusions you choose to draw and your actions resulting from those conclusions) can make you a bitter and lonely person.

6. Happy people experience solitude as a healthy and necessary part of life. As a so-called "stresspert," I am regularly asked whether life today is more stressful than in times past. Of course, anyone who presumes to answer such a question has already begun to think too highly of himself. Nevertheless, I try always to grapple with this question. Far be it from me to compare the stress of the Jews in Warsaw or Dachau in 1940 to the stresses of American urban life in 1990, but I do believe the normative stress of those of us living in American cities today is different from those prior to the information revolution. We suffer from sensory overload. Our senses are bombarded with data, too much for our brains to assimilate. We are, therefore, unable to think deeply about anything for very long. Distractions, televisions, telephones, make us easy targets for those whose livelihood depends on directing our attention to their product or service.

We are all interdependent. We have made ourselves dependent on each other, for the water we drink, the toothpaste we use, and the energy that operates every gadget in our house.

And we habitually depend on these services, so much so that when something breaks, when service is interrupted, we are disabled for hours. The interruptions in our lives result in hostility and even depression.

While we can improve our coping skills for life in the twenty-first century, we are going to require time for retreat and the opportunity to utilize solitude for rebuilding our minds and souls.

7. Happy people take the initiative. They do not wait for someone to do something. I have found that I had rather take the first step and let others respond than to always be responding. When you take the initiative, you set the course of events. When you make decisions, when you take action, the momentum is on your side. When you have an idea, you can be sure someone has already had it; but if you *act* on that idea, you may be surprised how few people put their ideas into action. Fear of failure inhibits most of the population. Happy people will not be found swimming in the wake of others' ideas. Happy people take responsibility for their future and do not leave their lives in the hands of those who may or may not share their values in life.

8. Happy people are flexible. They take interruptions, the unexpected, and bend without breaking. Having a sense of control of your life is important, but having to be in control of every moment of every day will leave you exhausted and angry. Every sailing buff knows she doesn't control the direction or intensity of the wind. Yet she learns how to reach the destination using the prevailing winds. Nor does the white water rafting crew control the powerful rapids. They use the relentless current to control the raft. Happy people don't exhaust themselves fighting life's currents. Instead, they use them to reach their goals.

9. Finally, amazing as it seems, happy people never seem to be looking for happiness. Happiness is a relative and elusive

term. It seems to be a by-product of a balanced life. It is not what we set out to achieve as much as something that one day, in a quiet moment alone with God, we experience. From the planets in outer space to the molecular structure of the body's smallest atom, the Creator seemed to have in mind "peace," that state in which there is balance. Not perfect balance, for there is no such thing. But that point where there is an equalizing of tension. And, that is happiness.

We have much to learn as the children of God.
The most difficult, perhaps is to learn
    how to regard our trials and tribulations—
    even the tragedies that beset us—
    as capable of enhancing and enriching our lives.
Whereas God does not send them, He does permit them,
    and He can use them to draw us closer to Him
    and thereby accomplish His purposes
    in and through us.
We desperately need the wisdom to accept these
    painful happenings with graciousness, even with joy,
    knowing that whatever they may be,
    God can transform them from ugliness into beauty,
    from the plots of Satan designed to destroy
    into the purposes of God
    destined to do us good.
The key is a genuine faith in a loving God,
    a faith that frees us and strengthens us
    to endure whatever may come our way.
                        —James 1, *Epistles/Now*

7
Goldfish Really Do Die

"Dear Daddy,
   I just came in your office to see it for one last time as the way I remember it. I'm sorry all your devoted and unnoticed work had to end this way. I know God has something great for you because you are a great man. I'm very proud to call you my father. I've always been proud of you but this incident makes me even prouder. I just wanted you to know I'll always stand behind your decisions just as you have mine. I love you very much, Daddy.

Your little Doll,
Mydonna"

   My husband found this note from our daughter, whom he calls "Doll" to this day, on his desk following the forced termination—support from a daughter whose own world was disintegrating. The tentacles of forced termination move beyond the minister and his wife and pull their children into its circle of destruction.
   Children are surely as much victims in this crisis as are their parents. Their worlds are turned upside down, their belief system challenged. And they hurt because their parents are hurting.
   Our son and daughter were at different points in their lives

and had, as I've already mentioned, different relationships with me.

At the time of the termination, our son was already married and had small children. He was living in another state, attending one of our denomination's seminaries to prepare for a church-related vocation. He was also serving parttime on a church staff.

He had been a part of the church from which we were terminated. However, other churches in our ministry had also played significant roles in shaping his life. In other words, his world had been influenced by more than just that one church. Although he is no longer in a church-related vocation, he is an active layman in his church.

Our daughter was a high school student, and most of the responsibility for my care while I was ill fell on her. Our roles reversed, and she became the mother. Also, she had been a part of this church since she was a fourth grader. Her lifelong friends were there.

Her identity, in many ways, was taken from her. In fact, a counselor to whom we took our daughter told her, "You have been stripped of all your identity, your friends. Everything about your life has been stripped from you."

Now married and a mother herself, our daughter is an active member of her church.

Forced termination and our own particular family problems resulting from it and surrounding it affected my son and daughter differently, but both in significant ways.

The forced termination caused both of them to reevaluate their understanding of the church and their place in it. But, I am so grateful that both of them came through the experience with their faith in God intact—even strengthened—though it was shaky at times.

At my request, my children have contributed their own sto-

ries concerning how they saw themselves as members of a minister's family and what our forced termination did to their spiritual lives. As they share their feelings and experiences I realize,
again, how very personally forced termination affects each family member.

Perhaps their stories will help you better understand how
your children see their role in a minister's family and give insight into what they are going through.

Our Son's Story

"Our family life centered around the church. You always
seemed to be the wife and mother that staff members were suppose to have. Dad was a minister of music, and your talents in
music fit the bill. Dad believed in graded choir programs, so
you were great at children's choirs. Dad needed an accompanist
that could flow with him, so you played the piano and organ.
You could even sing so all of his songs didn't have to be solos!
Because Dad related to youth and you had good taste in up-to-
date fashion, you could relate to girls on their inner and outer
selves. Even though all of these were tied up in Dad's work, you
always seemed to give them your touch and make them your
'ministry.'

"As I grew older that view changed a little. A lot happened
during a three-year time period, and those things may have
been part of the cause. Part of it was a transfer of time and energy to your family. Mydonna and I were very active, and running
the household was a job. Also, you began to find a niche for
your talents in writing for the denomination. I'm sure that out-
let satisfied some of your desire to serve and help people. From
my perspective, your role in the church became a little less visible. Your help to Dad became more of a direct spouse support

and not as much of an assistant minister of music. That is not to say you were not a support to Dad's ministry. It is just that your focus seemed to shift slightly. The joy and fun of it seemed to be missing. With our last move, things at the church were new and alive and positive and you were moving back into the role of "sidekick" and vocational support as much as helpmeet (I hate that word!) and spouse.

"I was off at school, and so I was removed from Dad's situation and from yours. The headaches, the stomach problems, the nerves were all explained to me as either physical malfunctions, emotional weaknesses, or results from years of damage done in your past. I was told these symptoms were compounded by the termination.

"I never knew the depth of drug involvement or the inability to cope with reality. I guess I wanted to have a mom that could cope because you always had. I had never seen you or Dad in a position where there seemed no hope or future. I believe the Lord shielded me from a lot of that because it might have changed what I was doing with my life. If my family is hurting, I want to be there, and I might have quit what I was doing and come home. That probably would not have been good for either one of us.

"I think, for the most part, I can say that I never saw you as a wallflower staff wife that just stood beside her husband and watched his ministry go by. You had energy and abilities that allowed you to participate and supplement the work that Dad was doing. I don't believe Dad could have done the things he did without you.

"I also saw my role in the family in much the same way. I was involved in the work that Dad did as a helper and as an example of what a real Christian home should be. It was pressure sometimes, but I never regretted it. In some ways I believe it was positive. Not many professions in this world offer the children an opportunity to aid in the success of their father's profession. My life had a direct influence on the way people judged, not only Dad's fatherhood, but also his vocation. I always looked at it this way: If people could see a good relationship between Dad and me, then they would know that Dad could be trusted to help other children or youth and also be a loving, caring minister to them. I may have been overestimating my worth, but that is how I felt.

"It seems that families who have fathers in any profession that can change locations very often tend to live their lives more aware of the father's vocation and how it affects their lives. Every major change in our lives and every opportunity that any of us experienced was directly related to where Dad was in his profession. That is the constant. A staff family is there because of the church, and therefore the vocation and the church become the stabilizing force.

"My initial reaction to the forced termination was to fight. These people were interfering in God's plan for Dad's life, and it wasn't fair! I was left with a feeling that God somehow could have brought the truth out into the open, but He didn't. I still don't know if it was God's will for Dad to leave, but I believe God has blessed Dad in many ways for his response to the forced termination.

"For me, it challenged many of my ideas about how God protects us. I guess I believe now that He doesn't 'protect' us in the way that I thought. His protection is not a bubble He places around us, but a pillar that is built within. While things may hit us from the outside, we will not collapse because the pillar will hold. For that reason, I believe that my personal relationship with God has been strengthened. That has happened only through time and constant reassurance that God is guiding day by day.

"My view of the church and how it operates is a different

story. In many cases, I see that the political aspects of the church
have gotten in the way of the family, ministry, and community
aspects of the church. The church is not a family anymore. It is a
bureaucracy, and in any political situation, egos and power
plays become more important than ministry.

"I once felt that if God was going to make an impact on our
world, it would be through the church. My life revolved around
the church. Now I see that God will be God, in spite of the
church. The church has turned so inward that God is going to
have to go into the world to impact the world. I will go so far as
to say that this belief in the role of the layperson has contributed
to the fact that I decided not to pursue a career on a church staff.
I think that my options for ministry are much broader outside
the church. Even now, it hurts me to say that, but that is my
current perception."

Our Daughter's Story

"I don't really remember when or how Mom changed, because it happened so slowly. Dad was confused and didn't understand Mom, and she was usually under the influence of the
latest medication.

"The first problem I observed were her headaches. They
were so bad that she couldn't open her eyes, be in the light, or
even sit up. Dad has never known what to do when someone
was sick, and I was the only other one there, so I became Mom's
nurse. Dad was very tender and patient, although he didn't understand how to take care of a sick person. She slept a lot those
days. She would get up early and go to work, come home in the
afternoon, take a nap, eat dinner, and then go back to sleep. It
was her escape.

"There was the time I had been on a retreat and returned

home to find Mother in the hospital for tests. I went on home and started baking a cake for a friend's birthday. When I got to the icing, I ended up short. I just broke down crying. I know now that I wasn't crying over the icing. I think all my bigger frustrations and pressures got dumped on that icing. I just didn't have any strength left. By the way, Dad got me some more icing when he came home, and everything worked out fine.

"The next day I came down with the flu. I stayed home for a week trying to take care of myself while Dad worked and Mom was in the hospital.

"I remember my senior year in high school. I was working part-time in a doctor's office because I only had to attend school a half day. Dad had finally taken the job he has now. Mom had one of those headaches and had been out of work, and she was starting her problems with her stomach. The doctor had prescribed some new medication that made her act rather strangely. I was supposed to go to work on one of these days, but I soon called and told them I couldn't make it.

As I was getting ready that morning, I found Mother in Dad's office with his calculator in her hands. She was pushing all the buttons and growing more frustrated every minute. I asked her what she was doing, and she said she was trying to call her brother Dan. She said she couldn't make the phone work. I took the calculator from her and told her that I would make the call for her. I asked her for the number, and she handed me a piece of paper with scribbling on it that I could not understand. I put her back in bed. She never remembered one thing about that day.

"My senior year was one of the worst years of my life because of losing my church home, my friends, my father's identity, and seeing Mom and Dad hurting. I'm not sure if I will ever fully understand the meaning of everything that year, but the Lord has revealed many truths—truths that have strengthened all of us.

"I went away to college. I had some problems that year, but Mother was always strong through them and collapsed later. By the time I came home to work for the summer, Mom was very sick and the doctors needed to operate. She had been in the hospital a few times that year while I was in school. She never wanted me to know that.

"I can't remember how many times she changed medication, but with each one, she changed personalities.

"I remember coming home after I graduated. I was engaged to be married, and Mom and I were working on wedding plans. It was very strange at first to be with Mom because it was after her surgery and she was free of medication. She was energetic, awake, and had a mind of her own. It took me awhile to figure out why I had a hard time understanding her. It finally dawned on me that for almost four years, I had been the mother and she had been the daughter. I wasn't used to having a mother, friend, and supporter. Mom had changed. She was in control again. She had finally come to grips with the whole thing— church, her health, and going through changes in each family member's life. It was strange, but nice, to be the daughter again and to see Mom and Dad loving and enjoying life.

"All the years of separate churches on Sundays, no church on Wednesdays, nursing Mom, and Dad's silence finally came together in a wonderful strength that has only gotten better through the years.

"All of the revenge and hatred I felt for the church has come to be pity and sorrow. They made a mistake and acted outside of God's will. as a consequence, they nearly ruined three lives. But I've found that God's will does find its way through all of man's mistakes.

"I've learned there are limits to one's involvement in church and that church and staff are not always right and just, but God is. Maybe I needed to learn this to pass on to my children so that they can have a true and honest view of what church is all about. They need to know more than what others think about church and activities. They need to understand what God wants us to know to be the real purpose of church.

"In the last few years I have realized the effect the forced termination had on my reactions to the church and people in it. I did what author Chuck Swindoll says you do when you give up a fight or suffer pain: (1) Blame the one in authority; (2) Distance oneself from close Christians; (3) Doubt the truth taught in the past.

"First, I blamed all those people at the church for our problem. They did it, those hypocrites. That's all I could think. All those people involved were supposed to be deep Christian leaders.

"Second, I found I had built a wall between me and other Christians. I didn't trust them, and I promised myself I wouldn't be hurt ever again, not by the people in a church. I didn't get involved in a church for about four years. I felt the need, but I didn't even want to be expected to get involved. I didn't want to be made to feel guilty about anything. I have kept Christians at arm's length. I haven't really trusted them. I also didn't know if I would be accepted in a church. I had always been accepted as the minister of music's daughter, never just a member. I still find myself hesitating when getting involved, but I'm doing better. I still have my guard up.

"My blaming the church and staff really made it hard for me to respect any church leaders. I don't think the leaders of the church to which I now belong know how closely I have watched them. I am learning to trust staff members to a point for the first time in years because of the Christian attitude that these people have.

"Third, I began to doubt what I had been taught all my life about church, Christians, and the will of God. I questioned my role in the church, my commitment to the church. How involved is a person supposed to be without breaking down? I've learned God doesn't want you out of guilt. He wants you out of joy and dedication."

Others' Stories

"One of the deepest hurts," says Naomi, "is what this has done to my sons. They have become very disillusioned with Christian people who can so blithely inflict such deep hurt on fellow Christians. I pray daily that my boys will be able to put this behind them and once again serve in a church somewhere and nurture their Christian growth."

Says Mary, "Fortunately, our three children were all living in other places and away from this church in which they have their 'spiritual roots.' The only one we were really concerned about was our son. He had served as youth director on the staff and was now a seminary student, very deeply committed, and very sensitive to people's feelings, especially when they hurt. He had even served on the pastor search committee for the two years before he left for seminary. We prayed that he would not become bitter or disillusioned. We thank God that he survived without ill effects."

"We are a very private family and do keep our children informed about what is happening," relates Margaret. "I feel they have minimal scars. We had one child in college, one in braces, and we were making payments on a new car. Our bills were always paid on time. Of course, our savings were depleted and our college-age daughter took a year off to work and save for future expenses."

"Besides the pain my husband and I felt, we then had to tell our two teenage daughters and our families and friends," says Susan. "Our daughters accepted the news on the surface, but at the same time had deep feelings that they shared from time to time. Our older daughter, a junior in high school, said a few months later, 'Dad, you lost your job, but I lost my whole youth group.' She wanted to call our pastor and let him know in no uncertain terms her feelings, but we asked her not to do that. Our other daughter, a ninth grader, immediately got on the phone and called her friends and told them she wouldn't be coming back to that church.

"They cried over the phone as they talked. She adjusted to the new church fine, since she had a good friend there. Our older daughter resented having to change and has had a difficult time of adjusting. In fact, there are times when she stays home on Sunday nights or Wednesdays. This hurts. It's the first time in the life of our family that we have left one of our children at home while we attend church. We don't want our daughter to stray away from the church; we pray for strength for her and the decisions she will be making when she graduates from high school."

For a different look at the effects on children of forced termination, listen to the story of this one whose very beginnings were jeopardized.

"A letter from our church said they would continue the insurance since I was pregnant at the time of the termination," says Beth. "That insurance wasn't worth anything. I went to live with my parents and began looking for hospitals. None would take me because I was seven months pregnant. I went to General Hospital. I must have led a sheltered life. I've never seen anything like that place. It was dark and dreary. People were lying against the walls waiting for service. I said, 'Oh, God,

please don't let me have my baby in a place like this.' I eventually found another hospital where we made arrangements to have
the baby and leave in twelve hours in order to keep the costs to
a minimum.

"I felt cheated. This was supposed to be one of the happiest
times in our lives, but because of the church, it was one of pain.
I didn't like feeling that I was put in a shopping cart and
wheeled in and wheeled out in a few hours. My parents were
upset. They didn't want the responsibility of taking a newborn
into their home. We were told there could be complications.
We were also told to watch and if we suspected anything to
immediately bring the child back. We were very fortunate. Everything went well. We moved back and forth between our parents for the next several months. But our parents were supportive with food, clothing, and shelter."

"We protected the children by telling them very little about
what was happening," explains Robert (yes, we talked with a
man on this one!), who has experienced forced termination.
"We usually didn't discuss things at home because the people
who are trying to get you are the ones who are the children's
Sunday School teachers and so forth. When we did say anything, we tried to keep personalities out of it, keep it a general
situation. We kept individuals out of our conversations so the
children wouldn't hate the people who were after Dad. We did
tell them, 'We're going through a difficult time; Dad's having a
difficult time at work. But, this is a temporary thing we're going
through. We're going to go somewhere better.'

"We also protected our children by being very supportive of
each other. We maintained our family time, especially the vacations. I insisted that we take our customary two-week vacation.
We built some strong traditions which our kids (a daughter in
seminary training to be a counselor, a son who is a deacon, and a

younger son who is an active soul winner) still carry out today. We still rent a cabin on the lake and the kids still pile in with us."

Dan's Observations

The most important ingredient in the family's survival is not the parent's career but the family's love, mutual support, and belief in themselves, as well as a belief in God's care and guidance for them. In times of stress the best thing is for the family to believe in themselves and believe that they have the necessary resources for handling this stress.

All families have boundaries. How permeable that boundary is determines a lot about the health of that family. If the boundary is too tight and traps the people, they die, psychologically, from the inside. The family may self-destruct.

On the other hand, if there are no commitments and no loyalties, and people go out in all directions, that kind of family also disintegrates. A balance is what you are looking for.

Now, under adversity, the family will tighten the boundary. It's time to "circle the wagons," pull together, stick together. That builds a strong family. Ironically, when the crisis has been dealt with and is over, the family will wonder why they're not that close anymore.

A study conducted by professors at the University of Nebraska found six major qualities of a strong family. These are commitment, appreciation, communication, time, coping ability, and spiritual wellness. Spiritual wellness, as defined by this study, means that strong family members have a sense of a greater good or power in life, whether they go to formal religious services or not, and that belief gives them strength and purpose[1].

Of course, as Christians, we believe "spiritual wellness" fosters a strong family life. And, this crisis is a good time for one's spiritual life to bond the family. Bonding takes place as the family gathers on a regular basis for family worship and to pray for and support one another.

A parent's sincere, continued faith in God, in God's love and care for them, and in His concern for their ultimate survival and success, becomes the most important factor in the family's recovery. This faith in God can be expressed when a child hears a parent thanking God for His love and care and for the future, which is yet unknown.

Children take their cues from their parents. The best thing you, as a parent, can do is to develop your own sense of "okness" and confidence, because children will look to you to see how you are reacting to the forced termination crisis. When there is a trauma in the family, such as divorce, death, financial disaster, or forced termination, children tend to pick up the anxiety felt primarily by the mother. It is true that they follow the emotions of the mother more than of the father. This may be attributed to the amount of time spent with and the closeness they may feel toward the mother.

As I said, the more the parent feels confident about herself, the future, and God's hand in their lives, the better the children will be able to handle the forced termination.

I recall those kinds of comforting, reassuring statements made by my mother on several occasions when our family—a minister's family—moved. I do not remember being anxious about any of those moves. Mother had a sense of humor that made all of us deal with it.

The younger the children, the more their sense of security is invested in the parent. When faced with what I call an adversarial relationship with people outside the family, children seem to take it pretty hard. They may begin to see those people as the enemy, thinking, *Those people don't like my daddy or don't like my mother. Those people are all bad.*

Whenever a church must terminate a minister, it is important that loving, sensitive people represent their position to the minister and family. It is important that the church go far beyond the common termination procedures of corporations in providing security during transition. So often, termination is handled badly. Letters from numerous victims reveal deep scars resulting from insensitivity.

Termination brings feelings of rejection, humiliation, and embarrassment. Children are placed in a very difficult situation. They have to deal with children of church members and church leaders. They may see them at school, in Sunday School, or other church organizations. Children need to be helped to see these people, not as the enemy, but as people who have a difference of opinion and who view things differently than the family does.

This forced termination crisis is a good opportunity to teach children how to deal with relationships that are very, very difficult. This is tough, but I think we have to help children understand that a church is a group of Christians who have bound themselves together with a common purpose and who have organized themselves to serve what they believe to be God's will in the community and around the world.

The emphasis here is on the fact that the church is made up of people. Wherever you have people, you have the best that human beings can be and you have the worst that human beings can be. Church does not remove us from that reality of life and not to teach children this fact is to set them up for a grave disappointment later in life.

A pastor friend of mine once told me about an encounter with an acquaintance in downtown Fort Worth one day. This woman was carrying a water filled plastic bag in which a goldfish was swimming around. She explained to him that her daughter's goldfish had died while the daughter was at school and the mother was replacing it before the daughter returned home. This mother didn't want her daughter to know that her pet goldfish had died.

This is what happens when we perpetuate a myth. That goldfish live forever and that churches are perfect are both myths. We must explain to our children early on that church is where we go to experience fellowship with Christians, to worship and to learn about God. As my friend the late Gert Behanna said, "Church is not where I go to find God. It is where I take him."

The church is run by people who sometimes do wonderful things to minister and who sometimes make decisions that result in pain for others. It is important for children to learn this fact.

Just as we need to learn the difference between the church and God and our relationship to the church and our relationship to God, so do children need to understand that.

While reading this, you may have been wondering how you are going to help your children understand and accept all this when you may not understand or accept it yourself. The purpose of this book is to help you reach an understanding of what has happened to you and help you move ahead from this point.

You can do several things to help your children weather this particular crisis. Of course, a great deal depends on the ages of your children. The kind and amount of help you give your children will depend on their ages and how much impact the forced termination will have on their lives. Myra's teenage daughter represents one group. She was still living at home. She had grown up in that church, and much of her daily life was invested there. She also had to accept a great deal of responsibility during this time. Myra's son, an adult in seminary, represents another group. As his words confirmed, the possibility exists that the family's experience with forced termination could adversely affect the plans he had made for his life and the way he perceived his calling.

Young children represent another group, and you need to decide how much to tell them.

Because your children will continue to encounter friends from the church who will ask questions and make comments, they need guidance in making appropriate responses to these comments or behaviors from other children. For instance, classmate in Sunday School may ask your child, "Why are you leaving our church?" Your child might reply, "Because my dad will be looking for a new church, and this church will be looking for a new minister."

"Do you want to leave our church?" To this question, your child might reply, "No, but I know it will be OK when I make new friends."

Also, give your children time to adjust to the changes that will affect them and their daily life-style. Many times parents have months to adjust or prepare for the consequences of forced termination while they are trying to spare the child the "death of the goldfish." Then, at last in a few hours or days, the child is expected to adjust and accept all the adult decisions that have been made for him or her.

I'm not suggesting that a child should be involved in every stage of off again/on again discussions about termination, relocation, and other related matters. But a child needs some time to adjust to the changes while being reassured of the strength of the family, God's love and care, and the parents' confidence in the future.

Another thing you can do is maintain your family time and your family traditions as much as possible. Remember the man who said he insisted on continuing the family vacations? If you are accustomed to taking vacations, take them. If you go to a certain place every year, go there again this year. If birthdays are important parts of your family life, make sure they continue to be special times. Whatever your family does as a family, continue to do those things. When and if you move to a new location, move those traditions with you. Make sure there is continuity for the children and yourselves.

Pastor's wife, Barbara Hughes, says in the book she and her husband wrote, *Liberating Ministry from the Success Syndrome*:

> I make home and family a priority. During stressful times, some put family priorities on hold. This is a mistake and will eventually heighten the strain. By keeping things running smoothly at home, staying on top of the children's needs, keeping a neat home, preparing enjoyable family dinners, involving my husband in celebrating birthdays, and attending school programs, home remains for us all a place of joy and refuge rather than an added source of stress.[2]

How true! The home should be one's refuge. Within this setting children can learn that goldfish do die, and that there are other goldfish to enjoy.

It is obviously not our primary concern to be popular
with the people with whom we deal even though we are
charged with the task of loving and serving them.
We are, first and foremost, to please God, to serve Him,
and this may not earn for us the commendations
of the crowd.
It will, if we are faithful,
result in our Lord's commendations.
It is important, however, that we commend one another,
that we encourage and support our colaborers
in whatever ways we can.
The task is difficult; the road is rough for all of us.
We need, from time to time, the feeling of strong,
loving, undergirding arms to enable us to bear
the burdens of our respective ministries.
Indeed, the joy and strength that comes to us
in our labors will often come
in our love and concern for one another.
—1 Thessalonians 1 and 2, *Epistles/Now*

8
Where Do I Go for Help?

The pain, confusion, embarrassment, isolation, fear, anger—all those feelings brought on by forced termination—are simply too much to bear alone. You need other people with whom you can just talk and you need other people who can give you real help and guidance.

My response, instead of reaching out, was to withdraw into myself. After we were forced to terminate, I took more prescription medicine. I didn't want to think or feel. That's when my brother Dan, who lived too far away to be a constant presence, insisted that I find someone with whom to talk. Talking up front, early in the forced termination experience, can help avoid a real crisis later. He says you cannot put out a fire standing in it. You have to get out and get back from it. Friends, as well as professionals, can help you stand back from the fire.

Some people, I have discovered, cannot handle being around others with problems. There are those who simply cannot bear the pain. Others, who are probably not real friends anyway, realize that you cannot be helpful to them, so they move on.

Some people try to help, but their help is misguided. I heard so many times, "You are the fortunate ones. God has something so much better for you." I'm sure they meant well, but I hated hearing that. When you are hurting, the future seems so dim.

Fortunately, there were people around me with whom I

could talk and people who related to me in positive ways. Dan was the only family member outside our immediate family who really knew what we were going through. The others cared for us, but we did not share all that we were experiencing with them. Though Dan lived in another state, he has worked on church staffs, has worked with others experiencing forced termination, and he is trained to help people in crisis. However, he knew I needed people close by with whom to talk.

I've already mentioned I had one friend from the church with whom I could talk, and who would not judge me. However, I felt guilty about her continued relationship with me. I feared she could also be hurt and be "guilty by association."

Another friend paid for my airline ticket to go to my brother's clinic for counseling. I protested when she and her husband offered the money, saying, "I cannot take this." Her reply was, "Do not take the joy away from us. We want to do this." What friends!

Other friends who knew about the forced termination were afraid they would make things worse if they did try to do anything, and that is understandable. Most people are so astounded by such a turn of events that they don't know what to do. There were people in the church who wanted to help us, but, after the fact, there was nothing they could do.

Church staff ministers and their families tend to have most of their friends within the church, and I was no different. I've learned that we really need to have many friends, a support group even, outside the church so that our friends don't have to change if our place of employment changes. We can then have someone to rely on in a crisis.

One of my friends, involved in church work in another city, keeps a support group around her. She says she needs people who can hear her inside feelings and thoughts and they give her feedback. This keeps her from getting off on tangents. She points out, however, that being in a support group takes a lot of work, as does any relationship, on the participant's part. It doesn't fall out of the sky. Being in a support group involves a lot of give and take.

One pastor's wife, Virginia McAffee, wrote an article noting the need for a support group among people in her role, and I can attest that other staff member's wives have the same need. Says McAffee:

> Pastors' wives have failed to build up a sufficient support group among their peers. Having been all things to all people for so long, they hesitate to let down their guard, fearing being left vulnerable to further heartache.
>
> Pastors' wives need to come together to help and support each other, to share in the good times as well as the bad. God has placed us where we are for a purpose.
>
> Pastors' wives need to be ready to reach out to each other—not just to persons within their own church. Pastors' wives in the same association or city can help each other."[1]

One source of help was available to me, and I shall be forever grateful for this also. This was one advantage I had that my husband did not have. I had the people where I worked. I've mentioned already that I worked for a denominational publishing house, and people there were positive ingredients in my healing. These people gave me overt and subtle support during this time.

Many of these people did not even know about the forced termination (although I felt the whole world knew!). But by their kindness and consideration during times when I was ill or not functioning at my best, they helped me. Others did know and were willing to let me talk or, again, bear with me while I tried to do my job.

Also, my place of employment provides a staff counselor for

employees, and it was to this man that I went when Dan said I must get help. I would make my appointments late in the day so that I could take some sort of pill before my session. Of course, I was just in a daze. The counselor said I would start talking and just trail off into nothing.

He has since told me that he was afraid I was going to take my own life. If not that, he feared I would lose my job because of the prescription drugs, and if that happened on top of my husband losing his, he was afraid I would never recover.

The counselor said I had no feelings at all, and that's when it's dangerous. But, he said one day he finally saw anger and he knew we were getting somewhere. He still wondered if I would survive, but he didn't know the influence Dan's encouragement had on me and did not know the strength I had developed through my family life.

I am so thankful that my place of work provides such a person, and I am thankful that he let me talk, offered guidance, and simply helped me to hang on.

Of course, as you know now, I eventually received counseling from psychotherapists in my brother's clinic, and Dan is telling you in this book the things I learned there.

Others' Stories

"I have a hard time," says Naomi, "dealing with friends who come weeping telling me they didn't know what was happening until it was too late. I had talked with many of these people and made them aware of what was happening, but as one friend said, 'It wasn't that I didn't know; I didn't want to know.' We are grateful for the loving support and encouragement that has come from several of our former pastors and from others who have faced the same dilemma in their lives."

Says Jackie, "Different well-meaning friends have tried to 'love' us out of this, but even that is not the total answer."

"We have many relatives and friends," says Annie, "we have been able to share with and pray with, and two young pastors in our association have been of great help and comfort. The second week after the termination we visited with longtime friends and went to church with them. She teaches a ladies' class, and the lesson was on Colossians 1. As I read verses 9 and 10, I realized how this couple, our children, my stepmother, and other friends together with their respective church families (yes, and even friends in our own church) are praying for us in just this way. And we know they still are."

"We had support from the pastor and minister of education of another Baptist church in our city," says Susan. "They came to visit us and welcomed us into the fellowship of their church. We are thankful for this support and are glad to have a place of service.

"Both of our mothers (our fathers are deceased) were very upset and are concerned about our finances and wonder if my husband will be able to get another place of service," continues Susan. "As people in the church where we are now members find out about our situation, they have shared with us that they are praying for us. This has been encouraging. Some have shared that they have been through similar experiences, and they know what we are going through. The conference we attended at the Baptist Sunday School Board was very helpful. Just knowing that the Board is supporting us in this difficult time gives hope for the future."

"Our being in a Sunday School class together has been a nice experience," relates Margaret. "Our class has been there encouraging us, but not insisting that we discuss details. Several of

the members have been in a similar situation or are in one at this
time. Members of the (new) church were constantly 'checking'
on us in a quiet way to make sure our finances were in check.''

"People phoned or wrote to us as it began to dawn on them
what had actually happened," says Mary. "We appreciated their
concern. It helped, but all they could say or do could not remove the devastating hurt."

"It was a great comfort to me," says Beth, "to know that if
things were really tense around the house I could send my kids
over to my mother's house and she would spoil them and pam-
per them."

Dan's Observations

You do need other people during this termination experience. Everyone needs people with whom they can talk and vent
feelings during any crisis. You may also need more specific help
in coping and deciding how to move on from this point.

Some of your extended family members may be able to provide that unconditional acceptance you need during forced termination. A lot depends on their own maturity and the nature
of your relationship with them prior to the forced termination.

The toughest part for you will be watching family members,
such as parents, brothers, and sisters, become angry and bitter
at the church. You may be recovering long before they do!
Family members may generalize their attitudes from "that
church" to all churches in general. This is unfortunate as well as
unfair. Family members who have always been critical toward
churches may use this as evidence of their unhealthy conclusions regarding churches. You have enough with which to deal
without having to defend the very institution responsible for
the immediate crisis in your life.

Your love for God and continued faith in Him will serve as a witness to your family. The point is that for many people in your place the extended family might not provide sufficient help. You will have to judge for yourself just how much you can rely on them.

I encourage you not to give up your truly close relationships within the church because of forced termination. They may not be the enemy, so don't treat them like the enemy. There are people in the church who are close to you and who are totally shocked by the whole thing. They may want to do something and may be in a position to do something.

Because one part of the church has made a decision does not disqualify all those people who loved and cared about you before the fact and who will continue to love and care for you during and after the fact. They are trusted friends who may not only be supportive of you, but also are able to listen to your pain and frustration. They need to know firsthand the impact of forced termination on you and your family.

Of course, these friends in the church also may be hurt and angry and may have problems with the church. But you can walk through it together.

You also need to have friends and interests outside your church so that if your role in that congregation is taken away you are not left alone.

My last position before entering private practice was in a large urban church with high visibility across the nation. I resigned and began immediately training myself for my new career. I had been a curriculum writer and educator, traveling and speaking at denominational conferences all over the country. Suddenly, I was nobody. As I worked my way through graduate school, I realized that for the first time in my life, I was a layman. Four years passed before I noticed that I hadn't heard from any of my clergy peers. At the same time, my friendships and community relationships had broadened significantly.

For the first time in my life I was a *member* of a church. Always before, I had been either a minister or the son of a minister. I began to see how narrow my world had been. You grew up thinking you couldn't do anything outside this particular world. In the church, everybody loves you and everybody brags on you. But, this is not the real world. I attended Sunday School where no one knew I was an ordained, seminary-trained minister. It was fun. It was wonderful to develop new friends inside and outside of the church.

So then, if you can build outside relationships all along, per-hapsbe with people that aren't even involved in church (I realize that may sound like heresy to some!), you will still have some parts of your life intact if forced termination hits. It may be too late for you to build these kinds of friendships as a support during this particular crisis, but it is not too late to develop them for the remainder of your life.

The church itself may or may not be a source of help for you. A church may represent either extreme when forced termination is considered. It may be so cold, calculating, and impersonal that it abuses unintentionally. Or, it may be so supportive that it is immobilized and cannot make such a difficult decision or carry it out when necessary.

A church more than any other organization in our society needs to be caring, supportive, and loving, especially during an experience such as this. It is not inconceivable that the same church responsible for the forced termination may be a supportive resource during this time.

Churches should provide appropriate monetary support, including such things as insurance coverage, for a period following the forced termination. Some churches do this, some do not. Others say they will, but things are not handled properly, and what actually is done is not what was promised. It is particularly distressing that many churches do not provide health insurance for those forced to terminate. Corporate America offers a lengthy grace period in which insurance is extended and the company even pays that health insurance for the terminated employee.

Churches should pay for counseling and career assessment for the one terminated and for his family. Even when a termination is necessary, the church should be Christian in its handling of the matter. Be sure to explore thoroughly any health insurance you may have since it may very well provide payment for counseling, a source of help that I highly recommend.

If your church does not or will not pay for counseling, seek ways to finance it yourself. Many people say they do not have the funds for counseling when they have assets, saving accounts, trust funds for children, and many kinds of things that have been either inherited or acquired through the years.

Now, I am not assuming at all that ministers have great resources; in fact, your money is probably very tight right now. What I am saying is to look creatively at the possible resources you might have. If your needs are serious enough, you may have to find a way to finance counseling.

Many counselors charge on a sliding scale, according to what the person is able to pay. Also, you may be able to reallocate some of your finances or sell or do without some unnecessary things in your life. Let me encourage you to explore all avenues to find ways to enable you to pay for counseling.

People going through forced termination can benefit from professional counseling. In fact, I unquestionably recommend that you seek family therapy. You may hesitate. You may be thinking, *Things aren't that bad.* Once therapy or counseling had a taint of mental illness attached to it. That is no longer true.

Counseling does not necessarily imply serious mental health problems. I regularly remind my clients that I am not some authority about to pronounce them sick or well. I do not cure people. A client typically hires a consultant to help her understand options and make choices. This consultant works for the client, not vice versa. In this sense, you may fire your counselor or therapist whenever you desire. This is why the stigma of counseling is rapidly being replaced by a status symbol in some communities!

Counseling by a licensed/certified professional who is trained and experienced will help you prevent such a crisis from resulting in serious, life-threatening mental health problems requiring psychiatric hospitalization. A destructive family system, like cancer, is treatable if detected early.

One speciality in the mental health field that has done more than any other to remove the stigma attached to counseling is marriage and family therapy. Forced termination, as in any other major crisis in the life of the individual, affects the entire family. Those of us in the field of family therapy know that the family is a system that is well-defined, with rules and boundaries that are often never stated but nevertheless guide the entire family. All families have roles for each member. When the family does need help, they need to receive it from someone who can understand the impact such a crisis can have on a family. A family therapist is trained to detect the impact forced termination has on each member of the family, even those members not verbally expressing the pain.

Professional family therapists are trained to diagnose the system and treat the family without "taking sides" or blaming. The professional objectivity is part of the condition in a healthy therapy setting. Good family therapists will not reject the church.

Also, you need not fear that the confidences you reveal to your counselor will soon be known all over the community. A good family therapist, as well as a well-trained mental health professional, is required by credentialing agencies to maintain confidentiality. In most states a client's confidence can be broken only by court action, life-threatening conditions, or in issues involving the welfare of a child.

Much confusion exists in the public regarding the categories of mental health professionals. This is due to the growth of the mental health field and the many specialities now available.

A **marriage and family therapist** has emphasized these particular relationships in his or her training and knows predictable cycles in both individuals' life span and in the relationship in which they are involved. Sex therapy is a specialty often included in this profession.

A **social worker** has knowledge of both group dynamics and individual human behavior and has learned skills to enhance the relationship between individuals and the community or people surrounding them. Social service agencies operated by your city or state are often publicly funded and may be an affordable way to obtain counseling.

A **psychologist** has special training in measuring aspects of an individual's personality or behavior and interpreting the difference from similarities to the majority of people. Psychologists may specialize in marriage or family psychotherapy.

A **psychiatrist** is a physician and is the only helping professional qualified to prescribe medication. Some psychiatrists will specialize in family treatment also.

A **pastoral counselor** is an ordained minister with training and supervision in professional counseling. Pastoral counselors may work in church-sponsored counseling centers or as a staff counselor in a local congregation.

A **professional counselor** is usually licensed and certified by state and national boards to provide a wide range of counseling services to the public. Minimum requirements include a master's degree in the field with approximately a year's supervision after graduate work.

The name used to identify the therapist and the clinical memberships in national or international associations best identify the person's speciality, training, or expertise. National or international board certification implies a level of expertise based on training, board evaluation, and supervision at the highest level. Licensing, while important, implies a minimal level required by that state for that profession.

Be aware that even though a person is a licensed, certified professional, these things do not necessarily imply competence in family therapy. The national standard for marriage and family therapists is clinical membership in the American Association for Marriage and Family Therapy. The professional and his or her reputation still need to be checked out. Licensing and certification represent the minimum standards.

It is important that you find a therapist with whom you feel comfortable and that you trust. Friends or your family doctor may be able to recommend a counselor. Or, you may contact counselors directly and discuss with them the condition that makes professional help important. The crucial thing is that you seek objective, trained help.

The choice of counseling may be the wisest choice you can make, the best kind of help you can get during forced termination.

Whether it be physical pain or mental anguish,
    material loss or excruciating sorrow,
    this does not separate us from God,
    nor alter our relationship to Him.
It is when we accept and cling to what God had done
    for us through Christ,
    irrespective of our human feelings and frailties,
    that the very conflicts that beset us,
    and may even threaten to destroy us,
    become God's tools
    to grind and polish and temper our spirits
    and prepare us for loving and obedient service.
        —Romans 5, *Epistles/Now*
There is no way to test the authenticity
    of our relationship with God;
    it is by examining our relationships
    to our fellow persons.
When we are short on compassion and concern
    for our brothers and sisters,
    it is probably because we haven't fully grasped
    or experienced God's infinite love for us.
        —Philippians 2, *Epistles/Now*
Whereas our peers may regard us as weaklings when we
    respond in gentleness and meekness to the abuse that
    comes our way, our Lord has by example revealed this
    as His way of advancing God's kingdom and has
    challenged us to live and to serve as He did before us.
This is the way of love that drew us into the
    family of God;
    let us walk in it.
        —1 Peter 2, *Epistles/Now*

9
Forgiveness Can Replace Anger

Of course, I was angry at the way Frank had been treated and what had happened to him and to all of us. He would never knowingly hurt anyone. How could people hurt him? But, my feelings were too painful for me to deal with. Anger and a multitude of feelings ached unbearably if I didn't keep them in check. I simply buried feelings of anger the same way I buried my other feelings—I just "copped out." I did not want to feel anything, including anger.

As I said earlier, I had so numbed all my feelings that the counselor where I worked was worried that I would no longer exist at all. He says the day I finally showed some anger was the first time he believed there was hope that I might survive this crisis. What I said or did that made him see the anger remains a mystery. I do know I kept saying, "I could not stand to see Frank in this small church with five or six choir members. I hated going, but I felt Frank needed someone." Later, I will tell you more about this dear congregation and what this church has meant to us in the almost ten years we've been there.

Anyone who believes he or she has been treated unfairly and unjustly has a right to be angry, I suppose. It certainly seems to be a natural response. But, once I let myself feel anger, I had to decide how to handle it and what I would do about it.

Once again, Frank served as my example. Only once did I see

him display anger during this experience. It was brief and final. Instead, Frank's approach to those responsible for the forced termination was one of forgiveness.

Frank did chop a lot of wood for our fireplace during this time! And he made numerous trips to the driving range (a free one!) to hit golf balls. I accused him of giving each golf ball a name just before the force of his drive sent it flying down the fairway.

I can only describe Frank's forgiveness as Christlike. He felt no need for retaliation. He believed the entire situation was in God's hands. His strength and Christian spirit showed me that one could move through this crisis without having feelings of anger consume him. I saw that it was possible to handle the anger, and to do so without using medication. Through my husband, I saw a forgiving spirit rather than one of hatred. I thought, *If he can do it, I can do it.*

Sometimes we think forgiving is admitting we're wrong, or admitting defeat, or saying everything was my fault. In the early stages, I kept thinking, *God why don't you show these people that Frank was right. Why don't you let something happen that shows these people?* But, God doesn't do that. Frank said many times, "God in His own time." That become a familiar reaction when I expressed my own anger.

And, ultimately, I was able to forgive. But, I will have to be honest and say that my forgiveness was almost selfish. Forgiving "them" was for me; not for them. I realized that I could not get well unless I was able to forgive. I could not continue my life with any degree of vitality in it and, at the same time, hold onto the feelings of anger.

For me, forgiving the people who were responsible for Frank's termination and those people who, by their uninvolvement, let it happen, was a decision that I consciously made. I did not wake up one morning with warm, wonderful feelings of love and forgiveness for these people. In fact, I did not wait until I felt I could forgive. I made a conscious, willful, deliberate decision to forgive.

I will admit that this was selfish on my part. I wanted to get well. I forgave them because I wanted to do so. Forgiving is not easy; it's not automatic; and, for me, it was not a one-time thing. Every day I had to make a conscious decision about how I was going to think, act, and react in terms of those people whom I felt had wronged me.

But, I found that each time I consciously forgave, it became easier to do so. One day it became automatic. A time did arrive when I saw those certain people, and I realized I didn't have to overcome those angry feelings anymore. I did not have to make a conscious decision about how I would think and act toward them. It had taken six years for me to reach this point. Dan had told me that one day I would turn a corner and realize that I could do and feel certain positive things without having to think about the reaction. Each time that happened, I remember I felt a ton lifted and thought, *OK, this is what Dan meant.*

Forgetting was another matter altogether. I prayed to God, begging Him to please let me forget. Then Dan reminded me of the saying, "Don't throw out the baby with the bath water." There were many good things in our past, and I did not want to forget them. Indeed, I wanted to remember the good times.

Lewis B. Smedes, through his book *Forgive and Forget,* spoke words that were particularly helpful to me during this time.

The only way to heal the pain that will not heal itself is to forgive the person who hurt you. Forgiving stops the reruns of pain. Forgiving heals your memory as you change your memory's vision.

When you release the wrongdoer from the wrong, you cut a malignant tumor out of your inner life.

You set a prisoner free, but you discover that the real prisoner was yourself.[1]

Forgiveness is God's invention for coming to terms with a world in which, despite their best intentions, people are unfair to each other and hurt each other deeply. He began by forgiving us. And he invites us all to forgive each other.[2]

Others' Stories

"I was so mad at the rumors and the things being said and how my husband was treated. I remember lying awake at night wishing I could meet the pastor and deacons in a dark alley with a baseball bat and beat the dickens out of them without them knowing who I was," says Beth, who was pregnant at the time. "Then there were times when I wished something would happen to them individually to make them feel the way I felt. I wanted them to feel the pain they had caused me. But, you can't dwell on wishing bad things on them."

"Our main objective," says Margaret, "is to get through this without feeling bitter. Speaking of bitterness, this young pastor has 'accused' me of being bitter, but I can honestly say I'm not bitter, only incredibly hurt, which he cannot possibly comprehend. Who can, unless they have gone through a similar situation?"

"One of the things I've learned through this experience," says Mary, "is that harboring bitterness will make spiritual (even physical) healing impossible."

"First, I was angry at the injustices of everything that occurred, and this for me extended even to God, I'm ashamed to say," says Jackie. "Personally, it has taken me a lot longer than I ever dreamed to even think halfway calmly about all this, and when I see those people that were hurtful to us at the mall, stores, and so forth, I still find it very hard to smile and say hello."

"I went through a period of disbelief, hurt and anger," says Annie, "but when church members called or came by to tell us how sorry they were about what happened, I told them it was all right, the Lord has something better in the works for us. He knew what was going to happen before it happened, and He would see us through. I felt for the people who were involved in causing the forced termination, glad I don't have to answer to God for what they did. I still feel sorry for them. One thing that has helped me a lot is that now when I think about them and become angry, I stop and pray for them by name, asking God to forgive them and use them for His glory. It helps to take away some of the anger.

"Patience has never been my strong point," she continues, "so over and over I have had to read passages such as Psalms 37:7-8,34; and 40:1-4,17. I kept my Bible open on the coffee table at these verses and read them over and over every day: 'Rest in the Lord; wait patiently for him to act. Don't be envious of evil men who prosper. Stop your anger! Turn off your wrath. Don't fret and worry—it only leads to harm. Don't be impatient for the Lord to act! Keep traveling steadily along his pathway and in due season he will honor you with every blessing' (Ps. 37:7-8,34, TLB).

"I'm still not patient," explains Annie. "I have my times of questioning God. 'God, do you know how hard it is to be patient? To stop being angry? To not worry? To be forgiving? Why don't you do something, *now*? I am trusting you, I know you are able and your timing is always perfect, that your Word promises you will take care of us and supply our needs, buy why can't it be NOW? Why do we have to sit here on the shelf, not able to accomplish anything for you? What good are we to you like this? If you aren't going to use us again, why not just take us home to be with you? We have done everything we know to do and nothing has helped, what else are we to do? What are we leaving undone?' Over and over these questions fill my mind. I don't have answers to them, but I have the assurance God does.

"There have been some Scriptures that have helped. Ephesians 4:23 says, 'be renewed in the spirit of your mind [attitude]'(KJV). When we have been through a forced termination, we are hurt, angry, frustrated, and want to get back at those who have hurt us. We need to work at this renewing of our attitude.

"In Colossians 3:13, Paul wrote, 'Bearing with one another, and forgiving each other' (NASB). Back in the early 1970s Harold Songer prepared a Bible study *Colossians: Christ Above All.* On page 107, he said some things that have helped me tremendously on forgiveness.

> Forgiveness is frequently associated with forgetting, and many Christians have suffered under the exhortation they are to "forgive and forget." . . . But to say that one has not forgiven until he had forgotten is to speak an untruth. When a person has been deeply hurt by another, he cannot easily forget. Forgiveness will not wash the painful memory away, but it will keep the wound form widening into a chasm that separates . . . Forgiveness is an attitude of heart and mind toward others. Not only should the Christian forgive his brother many times, but the Christian must forgive his brother many times for the same wrong. When one remembers the offense, the old anger, hurt and pain return and the Christian must forgive again.

"My husband is angry at God and man," says Winona.

"I expected to feel a good deal of bitterness toward the pastor, but surprisingly, I don't feel this bitterness," says Naomi. "I just feel pity that a group of good people can be so easily led."

Dan's Observations

Anger is the most powerful ingredient in your response to termination. You are angry. You've been forced to leave your job, as well as your place of worship and service, against your will. Your life and the life-style of your family have been dramatically interrupted. This is not what you wanted right now. Others have made choices for you that you would not have made for yourself. You are hostile!

Anger resides in the affective domain (see the triangle drawing on page 97). Anger is a feeling. In the affective domain, we experience stress primarily in three categories: hostility, anxiety, and depression. I define hostility as extended anger.

Anger can be useful as a natural reaction to abuse. However, anger out of control is a dangerous emotion. It must be handled properly. While anger resides in the affective domain, it must rely on the cognitive domain to regain balance. If you deny or suppress your anger, over time you will become depressed. When a person hates and suppresses that hostility over a significant period of time, this energy turns into depression. Experienced therapists know that, by far, the most common source of depression is hostility suppressed (a conscious process) or repressed (an unconscious process).

It makes you sick. In a recent article in the *Journal of the American Medical Association*, an exhaustive study of depression revealed it to be second only to heart pain and advanced coronary artery disease as the most disabling illness an employee can experience. Depression causes so many negative things—physiologically, emotionally, spiritually, and interpersonally. From any direction you choose to view it, depression is a destructive force.

Following a public discussion of repressed hostility, a participant asked me, "How can you block anger unconsciously? How can you do it and not know it?" The answer lies in understanding suppression. If you've practiced suppression, conscious avoidance, or denial long enough, it is like all other habits. You don't have to think about it. It becomes your "automatic" response to any stimulus or triggering event that ought to elicit anger. (See illustration on next page.) The alarming factor here is that when a person reaches the point where Myra was, she doesn't know when she is blocking anger. While there is a tremendous intensity at a time like this, it turns into depression because there's no release and no perceived way of processing it.

How do you do suppress anger and not know it? You do it the same way you learn to drive a car, by consciously thinking through each step and, over time, learning to drive to your destination without ever recalling turning, giving a signal, or braking. What began as a conscious process has become "automatic." This is why it is necessary to uncover the unconscious thinking or beliefs held in the unconscious and deal with these beliefs since they are the foundation for the depression.

A good therapist will seek out the healthiest part of a client, no matter how tiny that seed may be. Myra was just healthy enough to recognize her anger and know that in time it would destroy her. Her will to live was stronger than her need to hold on to the anger. We are *never* without resources. The same energy it took for Myra to hate was redirected into energy to live, to beat this thing, to get past it.

Anger must be handled in a manner that is acceptable to society and also healthy for you. We can fantasize for a while, but we cannot do what we would like to do to express the anger.

The diagram below shows the cycle which leads to the unconscious blocking of anger.

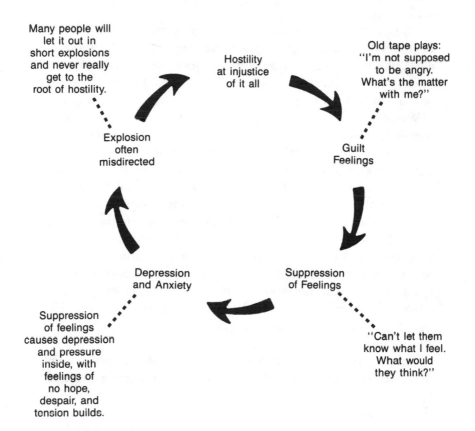

Many people will
let it out in
short explosions
and never really
get to the
root of hostility.

Hostility
at injustice
of it all

Old tape plays:
"I'm not supposed
to be angry.
What's the matter
with me?"

Explosion
often
misdirected

Guilt
Feelings

Depression
and Anxiety

Suppression
of Feelings

Suppression
of feelings
causes depression
and pressure
inside, with
feelings of
no hope,
despair, and
tension builds.

"Can't let them
know what I feel.
What would
they think?"

Remember the refreshingly honest minister's wife who said she would like to get the wrongdoers in a dark alley and work them over with a baseball bat?

In the early days of my practice, mental health professionals taught people to vent anger. It was very popular to encourage individuals to express that anger in a physical way but in a controlled setting.

I'll never forget one such counseling session that I conducted. I had designed a superb group therapy room with expensive wall coverings, including a ceiling to floor mural of an enticing forest with the sun shining through the trees. I placed a young woman in this room with instructions to express her anger.

When I returned, the room was in shambles. The inflated punching clown, a popular therapy tool in those days, was ripped to pieces and sand from its base was strewn wall to wall. For years after the cleanup, as I would lead therapy groups in that room, I had to look at gashes in my beautiful mural.

The worst part, however, was that the young woman returned only a few weeks later for another hostility therapy session! That's when I started a new approach. That form of therapy proved to be the most short-lived of my early career. But there was a better reason for changing my philosophy. Anger has a biochemical, hormonal element to it, represented by an influx of epinephrine (adrenaline) into the bloodstream. The body is not equipped to handle excessive sustained quantities of adrenaline.

There is mounting evidence that the most dangerous element of the stress-prone personality is anger. We now know that hostility is the culprit in the Type A personality that carries the high risk of heart disease. While physical exertion does help to process this adrenaline, it holds little value unless the source of the problem is addressed. There is an alarm center in the brain that instructs the adrenal glands to pump this hormone into the bloodstream and distribute it to the "action" points of the body, providing the energy necessary for fight or flight, hence the name "Fight/Flight Response" (FFR).

I do not want to minimize reasonable physical exercise. Programmed exercise with the consent of your physician is vital. However, if the mind, which is the source of stress, is not reprogrammed to alter expectations, then no amount of exercise will be adequate to process all the adrenaline being created. Once again, the cognitive holds the key to your destructive emotions.

Therefore, in order to deal with the underlying cause of your anger, you must look at your expectations of life. Are they realistic or unrealistic? If the mind is continually holding on to unrealistic expectations, hostility will be the outcome, no matter how much you exercise, talk, or whatever physical activity takes place.

My model for dealing with anger is to draw a simple diagram in the shape of a capital *I* (see next page). Across the upper bar of the diagram, write the word *expectations*. Along the bar at the base, write the word *reality*. The distance between expectations and reality represents the potential intensity of the hostility. As the expectations rise, the potential for hostility increases. As expectations are lowered, the potential for diminishing hostility occurs. If reality rises to meet the expectations, there is very little room for hostility.

So how do we reduce the distance between the reality of our situation and our expectations about how we think things should be? The human condition is such that people are fallible. People always see things from their own perspectives. People are predisposed to look out for themselves and their own self-interests. That may sound selfish, but looking out for oneself is not altogether bad. That's natural. There is innate in human beings a natural, healthy need for self-preservation.

This remains true when a person becomes a Christian. I be-

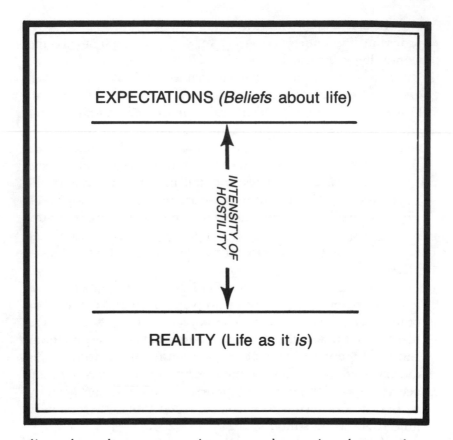

EXPECTATIONS *(Beliefs* about life)

INTENSITY OF HOSTILITY

REALITY (Life as it *is*)

lieve that when a person is converted, a major change takes place. She makes a commitment to God which will reshape her values. But, if she's been cursing profanely for fifteen years, for example, she is not likely to get up off her knees and never say another curse word. It usually takes time to change some of those habits. So, I believe conversion is a decision, a statement of intent, a declaration of what that person, who now belongs to God, intends to do. Frequently, it is accompanied by deep emotions.

What a Christian brings to this basic human need to preserve self is a balance between taking care of me and the joy that comes from ministering to others. Sometimes, these things get out of balance in our churches. Sometimes, self-preservation becomes the main intent.

Am I suggesting you lower your expectation of churches and say that "They are all louses, so I'll just expect them to be louses"? No, I am not. The church is God's means by which people attempt to minister in the world and be a redemptive force in the world. In the process of doing so, people who make up the church are human and they make mistakes. They frequently act out of self-preservation. And, many times, people are hurt by that.

Do you remember that we said earlier this forced termination experience is a good time to help your children understand that the church is made up of human beings who sometimes make mistakes? Now is also a good time for adults to understand the same thing!

Looking at a situation with realistic expectations and trying to see things from the other's point of view will help dissipate your anger. Try this exercise. Going through the physical motions of this exercise enhances its effectiveness, so pull up a chair. I've observed a dramatic breakthrough in therapy whenever I use this technique sometimes called "the double chair."

Briefly, in the double chair, the client sits in one chair facing an empty chair. The client imagines that the person who has wronged her is sitting in the other chair. In order to make it as realistic as possible, I have the client describe in detail the clothes—all the way down to jewelry and shoes—the other person is wearing, as well as the person's hairstyle and the expression on the other's face.

The client is encouraged, even prompted and prodded, to express the deepest feelings of anger and hostility towards the imaginary person we place in the other chair. Many times clients describe all sorts of bizarre things they would like to do to this "enemy." As the client begins to unload and as the intensity of her feelings begin to rise, I have the client ask the imaginary enemy, "Why did you do this to me?" or some such question that requires an answer and an interpretation of the events that led to the hostility and anger.

As soon as she asks that question, I quickly stop the client and instruct her to switch chairs. I tell her to assume the identity of the other person and to respond to those questions. As the individual, uncomfortable though she may feel, begins to hear that question asked of herself and she begins to role play the "enemy," an unusual thing begins to happen. That person begins to struggle with the answer, and many times she is unable to answer, but the very struggle brings about a condition which that person is experiencing for the first time. The client begins to understand the other person's perspective and intent. It broadens the entire range of responses that this individual has in regard to this relationship. As many years as I have used this method to enable the person to forgive and get past her hostility, I have never known someone who did not develop a different perspective after sitting in the other person's chair.

My point is that something wonderful happens once we gain the objectivity, once we, as the old saying goes, have walked in the other Indian's moccasins. Doing so leads to the conditions under which a person can forgive. Forgiveness is a very important part of the process of getting rid of the anger. As we get our expectations and reality closer together and begin to understand the other person, our feelings of anger or hostility lessen. We can begin to move into a position to forgive those who have wronged us.

Anger is a feeling (affective domain). Forgiveness is a mental (cognitive domain) decision on which you act. When you begin to understand the other person, you will feel less angry. You can then decide to forgive. Forgiveness is a statement of intent, and it is a process. A former pastor of mine included these words at the end of every worship service, "We are being redeemed." Your forgiveness will be that way. You may not be able as yet to say you have forgiven. But you can say you are forgiving.

For forgiveness to be legitimate, you have to see the other person as a human being, not with malice of forethought, not with the intent to defraud, not with the intent to harm. See the other as a human being acting out of his or her fears and self-preservation—and many times out of his or her own limitations and own abilities. Once we are able to see people as humans who are trying, but who are hurting us in spite of what their intent may be, we are then able to accept and forgive.

Whether these people were right or wrong is immaterial. As Myra discovered, anger is self-destructive.

It is important that you understand that people who maintain hostility over a long period of time are going to end up seriously depressed and badly dysfunctional, and they really are not harming the other person. They are not affecting the other person at all. What they are damaging is their own mental and physical health.

Much of the time, the other person is not even around to see your anger and resentment. As long as I hate someone or maintain hostility toward him, that person has gained control over me. Once I grant him that power, I have given him the privilege of controlling my emotions. Once again, expectations hold the key to forgiveness. If I no longer expect such and such of this group, then they can no longer have my hostility. Once I have altered my expectations of them (that is, "They will act unfairly sometimes.") and once I alter my expectations of me (that is, "I don't have to secure their acceptance and approval."), they can no longer control me through the emotion of hostility.

More importantly, by hating or being angry, you are robbing yourself of energy because hostility is a tremendous waste of energy. This kind of energy is being wasted on a person who has long since forgotten the issue and has moved on to other things in life. When this energy can be freed up, you can begin looking to the future again, focusing on your positive traits, skills, and attributes that can be used to minister, to be of service in another place.

I remember doing therapy with a person one time who emphatically said she did not want to forgive. I asked her if she *wanted to want* to forgive those who had wronged her or hurt her. I asked, "Is there anywhere down in there the desire to want to forgive?" Many times, as illustrated with this client, a person is not ready to forgive. Once they understand the importance of forgiveness, I suggest their prayers be, "God help me to want to."

In my life, I've found it helpful to know that as imperfect as I am and as many times as I have failed others, God continues to accept and love me while He continues to expect the best out of me. It is this kind of love that I believe God expects out of us as we deal with each other—not a naive kind of "doormat" response that could be even masochistic, but a kind of love expressed in the words of Luciano du Crescenco, "We are each of us angels with only one wing and we can only fly embracing each other."

Remember the promise, "For I am convinced that neither death, nor life, nor angels, nor principalities, nor things present, nor things to come, nor powers, nor height, nor depth, nor any other created thing, shall separate us from the love of God, which is in Christ Jesus our Lord" (Rom. 8:38-39, NASB). We can *always* count on God's love.

We often hear the phrase "forgive and forget," and we've

come to believe one has not forgiven if she cannot forget. But, does forgiving mean that you will forget? To forgive someone does not mean you no longer remember the event. Something resulting in so much pain as well as so much growth is not likely to be forgotten. Forgiving does mean that the event has lost its disabling grip on your life. Because you are getting on with life, your energies are invested in new activities and accomplishments. As you do so, and as some success begins to come, the obsession with the terminating event dissipates.

God continually loves us and forgives us. As Christians, we are to do the same for each other. I believe God wants this kind of love from us. Even though you have been grievously wronged and the pain still rips through your spirit, you can rid yourself of anger and be a forgiving person.

In view of the fact that church membership cannot
     guarantee salvation and doesn't apparently meet all
     the spiritual needs of every person,
     it is not surprising that the institution is
     regarded with suspicion; and some people insist
     that they can fulfill their Christian responsibilities
     and maintain their faith by other means.
Perhaps they can,
     but they are hardly qualified to put down the church.
Though our Lord made no effort to organize
     an institution, the net results of His ministry of
     redemption include the gathering together of the
     redeemed; and, in a society where strength lies
     in unity, this eventually resulted in what we know
     as the church.
Made up of human beings,
     it is permeated with human error and disunity.
Nevertheless, it has been and continues to be the means
     by which the Good News of God's saving love is
     communicated to us, and through which we are enabled
     to communicate it to the world about us.
And it certainly ought to be, and is meant to be,
     a loving fellowship in which we can support and
     assist one another in the glorious struggle of faith.
                         —Romans 3, *Epistles/Now*

10
Identity Is More Than the Church

Who was I? I was Frank's wife. His job was on a church staff. Because I was his wife, practically everything I did was to help Frank in his work.

I even felt somewhat responsible for Frank's success. Everyone in the church had to like me, so I thought, or it would hurt Frank. You can imagine how exhausting that kind of belief can be!

One of Dan's pointed questions to me was, "When you walk into a room, how many people have to like you in order for you to be happy? If fifteen people are in the room, do you have to be fifteen different people?" He had zeroed in on a big problem for me.

This mind-set also fostered my intense involvement in Frank's work. I played the piano or organ, sang, led choirs, and entertained as my husband needed. Or did I do what I *thought* Frank needed?

Much of my activity was guided by the word *ought*. If I do something, then they "ought" to do so and so. These people "ought" to be this way. Or, I "ought" to do or be a certain way. Forget this ought business! I am learning also to forget about "they," those illusive people who guide our lives for us, but whom we never actually see or know. But, these ideas filtered into the way I saw my relationship to Frank's job.

My own success in the church work and my acceptance of the people there defined a great deal of my self-esteem. Some of this perhaps comes from a misunderstanding, which is frequent among religious people, about God's love. Although it may be at an unconscious level, many of us today still feel we have to earn God's love.

Another thing that bothered me a great deal while on a church staff was living the fishbowl existence. Everyone in the church knew such things as our salary and our life-style, and the fact that they could control these things to a large degree, made me very uncomfortable. Again, I was not a person apart from the church. Everything in my life was connected with the church. This only intensified the feeling that I was swimming around in a fishbowl.

When Frank was forced to terminate, I felt that everything I had done was worthless. With all my efforts I had failed. I had to understand and believe that just because someone thought my husband's ministry was no longer needed at a certain church did not mean that I was not a worthwhile individual. Doing so is difficult when you invest so much in someone else's career.

Through my brother Dan's wise counsel, I began to understand my self-worth. Dan said, "Myra, you have talent, beauty, and intelligence. This is your one shot at life. What do you want to spend it on?" (Everyone needs a brother like mine!)

Now, I really know and believe that I am a valuable person. God loves me unconditionally. I am a person who has talent, skills, and interests.

One of the things I remember doing was walking up the steps in our house, with my head held high. As I did this, I would say, "Myra, you are worthy. No one can get you down. I don't care who doesn't like you, you are a worthwhile person." Then I would go back down the steps and start up again, saying the same thing . . . over and over and over.

How fragile I was then! Even though I am stronger today, rebuilding self-esteem, for me, has to be done over and over when some things happen. But, I keep working on it because I want to keep on.

Who am I today? I am more self-confident. While I still work for a religious institution and I still participate in church and help my husband in his ministry, I have done other things too. Although I certainly haven't abandoned music, I am pursuing my interests and talents other than music. I have begun to see myself as a valuable person apart from my husband's job.

Now, let me be very specific about one thing. Never do I want you to think that I am against the church. I believe in the church and its mission. I am still active in a church. Yes, I still play the piano or organ, although for a while I could not do it at all and I had to move gradually into serving in that way once again. Attending worship and participating in the ministry of a church is very much a part of my life. My earlier interpretation of how I should relate to the church and my expectations of how I should be treated by the church contributed to my earlier feelings about church.

But, my being is not defined solely by the fact that my husband is a church staff member. No longer do I depend only on the church as the place to give me good feelings about myself. Because I have other pursuits in life that also use my skills and talents, I no longer put such a heavy burden on my husband's career or the church.

Someone recently asked me to define what I now think a "good" staff member's wife should be. She is one who has her own identity. She has a healthy view of herself—the "me as I am." I think it is only when we have a good identity that we can contribute to and support our husband's ministry and, at the same time, be honest to ourselves and our own calling.

One day I walked into the office of the counselor at my place of employment with the statement, "I've come to you as a well person." As he and I talked, an important thought came to me, and I shared it with him. "I've heard and read all these stories about people who have been through all these traumatic things and how they thanked God for taking them through that. If they had not been through these things, they would have never . . . and on and on they'd go talking about how wonderful it is to have gone through such and such crisis.

"I never had believed a word of that kind of stuff. But, I can sit here now and tell you that I thank God for taking us through it the way He did," I told my counselor. "If not, I would have never known what these people were talking about. I would still be this sick person plodding along in the oughtness of do- ing all things. In the process, I would still be bitter and thinking that other people were putting all this on me. I would still be thinking I had to do this or I had to do that.

"If it were not for our forced termination experience, I would not be the person I am today."

The counselor said to me, "That's a sign of wellness."

If we know who we are, and as the saying goes, "Whose we are," then we will not be devastated by forced termination. One group of people somewhere cannot define our lives for us. They cannot evaluate or assign to us our worth.

Others' Stories

"To sum this all up," says Lucille, "we are learning to like ourselves as we are. We have nothing to be ashamed of. We all have a strong faith and we are each sharing in our churches. God is real and God will take care."

"Nineteen years ago my husband was called as minister of music and youth," explains Naomi. "It was a sure and definite call. It was the kind of call that we felt God's leading so keenly that I didn't even have to ask my husband what he had decided after we visited the church. I knew this was the place God wanted us, and from all indications, the church felt as sure as we did.

"We participated in every phase of the church program. I was involved very deeply in the church program, sometimes serving in leadership roles, sometimes in the role of participant, depending on whether or not I had leadership ability in that particular area and whether or not I was asked to serve in a leadership position, but always feeling a part of the church and not an employee or employee's wife.

"As our boys grew older, I took on more and more responsibilities in the church, especially in the youth ministry. At the time of his resignation, I was assisting weekly in two children's choirs, serving as puppet director, teaching an older children's Sunday School class, and directing special drama presentations from time to time.

"My husband was carrying a full load of activities in music and youth as well as doing hospital visitation once a week. These activities required him to be at the church daily for a minimum of eight hours and at least two hours five nights a week. These numbers of hours are not important other than just to show how very deeply we were involved in our work. For sixteen years it was a joy to serve our church and our Lord, and the people seemed to love us and appreciate the efforts we were putting forth.

"For a year we continued under these circumstances (problems within the staff which created problems within the church body), feeling that the Lord still wanted us in this church, yet despising the sense of 'taking sides' that was developing. I continued working very hard in the areas where I was involved but always having the feeling of 'how do the people with whom I am working really feel about me.' This created severe emotion-

al strain for both my husband and me. We were physically exhausted because of the constant hours and emotionally drained
from the divisive spirit that had been displayed in our church.

"I look back upon our experiences and see many feelings that
I have had. I lost a good deal of self-esteem as we went through
the period of criticism and divisiveness," concludes Naomi.

"We were not the first staff member to be terminated," says
Margaret. "My husband is now a junior high band director, and
I am working full-time in an insurance office. Two new careers
at our age are demanding, but also fulfilling."

"It has been exactly one year since 'our' termination," says
Mary. "I say 'our' because for thirty-eight years my husband
and I were a team sharing the musical ministry in every way."

"For four months after the forced termination," says Susan,
"my husband did not want to go back into a church staff position. We both have a deep sense of calling and today we are
seeking to serve the Lord. We hope and pray that someday we
will be back where we know we belong."

"I came from an emotionally abusive home," explains Justine. "My 'family' was my church. That's where all my 'pats on
the back' came from. I learned early in life that being sweet,
looking pretty, and being good was what brought me acceptance from the world. So when my husband was fired from the
church, my 'family' kicked me out—total rejection. My substitute family had told me they did not love me, no matter how
sweet, how kind, how hard I worked!

"It will be a long time before I will be able to open up to
people, to let them know the 'real' Justine. In the meantime,
I'm enjoying my real family—my son and daughter. I've
learned to do things for others because I want to serve the Lord,
not because I want people to like me."

Dan's Observations

The whole area concerning the role of the minister's wife is controversial. An entire book could be written on this subject alone!

Many ministers' wives believe their whole purpose in life is to support their husband's ministry. This is especially true of the "older" generation of women who were raised in a culture that said the husband and his career come first.

Other ministers' wives, especially younger women, do not see their lives wrapped up in their husbands' ministry. They have their own lives, their own careers that they have chosen to follow. I believe a career for the minister's wife could offer many advantages. Perhaps churches have unknowingly contributed to the two-career minister's family by not providing a salary comparable to other professions or executives in the community.

Wives are going to differ in their degree of involvement in their husband's career. We should allow a wide range of involvement based on individuals and their needs, and based on couples and what their relationships mean to each other. What is right and correct for one person and her husband may not at all be the best thing for the woman in another family. The crucial thing is that each person and each couple find what works for them.

But, saying all that, I do need to point out that no matter how supportive a wife is of her husband in the role of ministry, the wife should never lose herself so intently in the spouse's ministry that she has no identity apart from his.

If a woman's self-esteem is linked exclusively to her husband's career, sooner or later they are headed for trouble. Myra's self-esteem was unquestionably tied into Frank's career and his performance. She could enjoy a worship service only if they liked what he did. She was miserable if anything didn't go right.

A wife losing herself in her husband's ministry also can result in a negative impact on that couple's marriage relationship. When the wife is so intricately involved in his ministry, the husband will, in time, feel smothered. This may sound strange unless you have been there. But, when you are so lost in your husband's identity that you don't have one of your own, it becomes a burden to him instead of being a support system. It becomes pressure. The minister, in that case, eventually will feel trapped and will feel suffocated within that relationship.

Now that is what happens to the marriage relationship, but what happens upon termination to the individual who has no identity outside of her husband's? It is more than just a loss; it is a disintegration of the person because she has built no identity. She has built no sense of purpose in life outside of her husband's ministry. This wife simply must see herself as more than just a reflection.

Because one's self-concept is created so early in one's development, a poor self-concept is difficult to overcome. It must be your goal that you grow, that you continuously grow in your own self-appreciation. Accept those parts of yourself that are not strengths, while you work to make them strengths.

You have to value the goal of perfection, but while you are getting there you have a healthy, wholesome acceptance of yourself at whatever part of the journey you are on. You must enjoy the process. Accept yourself as a valuable person in the process of going from where you are now to where you can be.

I work at two levels with clients who need help with their self-concept. One of them is transference. I simply accept persons as they are. They come to accept me as an authority and a significant person who cares about them. They, in time and as trust builds, begin to feel better about themselves because there is a significant person who sincerely accepts them. Slowly, over a time period right for them and as their self-appreciation grows, I begin withdrawing and transferring more responsibility for their self-esteem to them. It is a bittersweet time when they no longer need me. That's when I know we both have succeeded.

Frequently, I have used my own journey of self-esteem as a pattern. I share with clients how I first came to accept God's acceptance of me. The first comment the Creator made after completing man and woman was "it is very good." And we have argued with Him ever since! I came to believe deeply that if the Creator pronounced us good, who are we to argue with Him?

The second level of therapy has to do with breaking the day-to-day habit of criticizing yourself, of majoring on mistakes. I grew up calling myself "Dummy" whenever I did something wrong. I believe I have broken that habit. Most of the time I don't treat myself like that, calling myself names. I wouldn't do that to my best friend, and I'm not going to treat his best friend that way. This sort of thing is a habit, and you have to break the habit of thinking badly about yourself.

One of the best ways to do this is to use cognitive exercises, including imagery. You practice seeing yourself as valuable and worthwhile.

I remember that Myra felt inadequate around certain people. She didn't want to be around them because these feelings intensified, frequently to the point of making her physically ill. However, confronting these situations was important in helping her understand and believe that she was as valuable as any of the people who intimidated her. She continually had to confront the situation, while at the same time reinforcing her own worth, until her feelings of inadequacy were no longer there.

I reminded her of situations in her past in which she was able to confront a problem or crisis effectively. She had succeeded then; she could succeed again.

Remember we pointed out earlier that because I'm her brother I could not become her therapist. There is a difference between a brother and a therapist. Here is this fragile person whom I love very much, and I'm giving her advice about confronting these difficult situations. She could get creamed! If I am only her therapist, I have a professional insulation about me, and I tell her, "Go ahead. You can do it." But, I'm her brother. I was her brother from birth, long before I became a therapist. I don't have that insulation when it comes to Myra. Her pain is my pain. I don't want to see her get hurt again, and I certainly don't want to be the one to push her toward more hurt. But, I had sense enough to make certain she had someone treating her who would confront and push her to the limits of her capacity.

That's the way alcoholic enablers operate in a family. They help a person stay addicted by avoiding confrontation. In one sense, they don't want to hurt the alcoholic further. But, by covering for them and by not confronting the issue, they are protecting them unconsciously and enabling them to remain dependent. In one sense the enabler himself has needs met by being the enabler, so it is very difficult to break out of this dysfunctional system.

Accepting yourself as a unique, worthwhile individual that many people love and that God loves will lead you to your core identity. Once you know and accept that person deep within you, you are then free to develop subidentities that are expressions of that core identity. You are not just a wife or just a mother or just someone's employee. These are subidentities, not your true identity. These identities are merely expressions of who you really are at the core of your being.

What are some of your subidentities?

You are a wife. In speaking about marriage, someone once asked me isn't it wonderful that two halves come together to make a whole? I replied no, I did not see two halves as a healthy relationship. It is much better when two wholes come together to form another whole, because when two halves are apart, they are merely one-half. When two wholes are apart, they are still whole. And, two wholes make a better whole than two halves.

There is a fine line between unhealthy dependency on each other and healthy interdependency. Nothing is more boring than to have someone, who has no life outside of you, depending on you. Conversely, nothing is more exciting than for two people to come together and share the excitement of what the rest of their lives can be like, what the rest of themselves is like. There is a vitality that comes to two individuals who have core identities that are not fused, that are clearly independent from each other, but that are clearly interdependent on each other by choice.

Frequently in premarital counseling, I sit face-to-face with couples committed to ministry and who are just starting out. I tell them not to expect their marriage to grow stronger and deeper just because they are sacrificially doing God's work in the church. Few professions have more pressures and expectations than that of the minister's family.

Because most ministers see their career as a calling and much more than just a career, some become wrapped up in "busy work" and forfeit the closeness and the relationship that should exist between a husband and wife. Obviously, if you "lose" yourselves in the ministry, you may lose everything, including the church. You do not need to be reminded which institution God created first, do you, marriage or church?

In order to grow together you need to spend time together. Go to places away from the church. Spend weekends (yes, weekends), as well as occasional weekdays, together away from church and children. Spend time away building and strengthening your relationship so that you can go back to the church with vitality and a kind of richness of mutual support that comes from your couple relationship.

Another important piece of advice for couples in the ministry is to live honestly. Do not allow the church to set you up for failure. I say this because our society has a bad habit of idolizing and setting up models. Whether it is a president of the United States, movie stars, sports heroes, or ministers, we have a need to set people up as models almost out of touch with the rest of us human beings. Then, we have the despicable habit of shooting them down. Do not allow a church to put you on a pedestal. Through sermons, correspondence, speaking engagements, and interpersonal relationships, let church members know that you are human and you identify with who they are and where they are. Avoid the ministerial phrases and seminarian terms that are overused and abused, and don't couch every decision and every behavior in spiritual terms. This will set you up for expectations that are totally unrealistic, to say nothing of the gap it creates between you and the nonchurch members you so much want to reach.

Staff ministers should not treat the pastor or senior minister as having more power or authority than the relationship suggests. Staff ministers should be assertive, direct, and they should expect to be treated in the same way.

The best example of finding one's own identity is in the life of my pastor. To me, the most powerful part of his ministry is his humanness. He and his family refuse to be set up for failure through unrealistic expectations.

I shall never forget the first Sunday School class his wife attended after they came to our church. I was teaching the class, and I made the mistake of introducing her as "the minister's wife." She quickly corrected me and said, "No, I am Rosemary." That made a tremendous impression on me.

In the years since, Charles and Rosemary have become my close friends. Through crisis after crisis in our church and in our families, I have watched as they defined for themselves what roles they wanted in our church. They did not, in any sense of the word, fit role expectations that the church had for them. And I watched them cut their way, literally weaving and slicing sometimes and painfully confronting members at other times, explaining that this is who they were, this is who they were going to be, and this is who the church could expect in the future from the two of them.

This couple has never made unrealistic expectations of their own children, and they have allowed each of their children to make healthy decisions on their own.

I encourage you who are ministers' wives and you who are the ministers to go to each church with the determination to be yourselves. But, you have to know who you are and be willing to be assertive, not to be confused with "aggressive."

Another subidentity you have is that you are a Christian. You need time to meditate. You need time when others, even your spouse, are not making demands on you. Interruptions—being on call all the time—prevent the kind of depth of thought that leads to creativity and to the enriching of a person's life through meditation and communication with God. I deeply believe in meditation. The only way you can have that is to guard private time and your schedule.

As a Christian, you must find the area of service in which you believe God wants you. While it is reasonable for any spouse to be supportive of her partner's career, as a minister's wife, you must find that balance between being supportive and being lost in his role. You need the option of saying no to responsibilities in the church while finding your own place of service to which you can give yourself without the feeling of "oughtness." You have interests and abilities that can lead to satisfying experiences through hobbies, activities, and/or a career, as well as church involvement and service.

I believe the Christian journey is about finding out who we are. One thing I want to emphasize about our own identity and our career choices is that God always wants the best for us. God never calls us to do something in conflict with the basic abilities, skills, and characteristics that are a part of our identity and personality. People who succeed in life are people who are in an environment that demands the skills they possess. When you are in a career or in an environment that demands or requires the skills that are strongest in your personality, you are way ahead of anyone in that same career field who does not have the skills and abilities demanded by that field. You are always going to be able to do those things that you do naturally with the most ease, with less energy, and with less inner conflict.

What are the characteristics that define your personality? What are the skills that naturally come from those traits and characteristics? A friend tells the story of her cousin, a pastor's wife, who had artistic talent. Through the years she developed that talent and began her own business in which she artistically decorated gift items made of wood. She also had learned to cut the wood into the different designs and patterns she needed. The artist said that one of the deacons at a church that was considering calling them found it unusual that the wife immediately checked around the pastor's home to see if there was a place where she could set up shop and cut wood!

What other subidentities do you have? What things bring you enjoyment and fulfillment? Think about these for a moment. How can you become involved in them so that your self-esteem is enhanced, so that you feel good about yourself?

A starting point to finding your own identity is to look at what other people are saying in a positive way about you. What do people say you do well? What are the ways other people continue to observe you as being different? What is it that you seem to do with ease that others may find difficult?

Myra has always enjoyed nice clothes and has a flair for fashion. She has done some work in the fashion world. Do you recall her son pointing out that she had helped teenage girls in their churches with their clothes? She was using her skills and talents to help others feel good about themselves. One of the things Myra has done since the forced termination was to take a course in makeup for television. Although it is not her primary job, she is a makeup artist for the religious television network operated by her employer. She is discovering her own talents and using them for her own enjoyment and enrichment, as well as helping other people.

Another way to begin to find your identity is to use your imagination. Christians tend not to do this, but it can be very helpful. Imagine that you have no restrictions whatever on you. Money, time, education, family responsibilities are of no concern. You have no restrictions to limit you. What would you do with your life?

Don't start qualifying why you can't do this. Think about what you want to do. No restrictions. Many times, when I ask people this question, they will come up with things they have been suppressing for years and years.

There is a certain minister of education I remember. In fact, I remember him very well. He wanted to be a counselor. And today, he is quite happy doing just that. Thousands of people have been ministered to by caring professionals on our staff. Many of them are people who will never walk into a church building. Each Wednesday for the past five years, I have talked live to a television audience from coast to coast, offering suggestions as to how they can find peace in their lives. Yet I still have someone occasionally ask why I left "The Ministry."

As a layman, a deacon, I have been able to accomplish more than I was ever able to do in my role as a minister.

My point is not that you should do what I've done, but that you should do what God has best equipped you to do. And if you do, whether that is as minister or as layperson, you will be happy, fulfilled, and successful.

Using imagination to picture what you would like to do with your life is important. When I say "no restrictions" many people immediately tell me why they can't do something. But, because of the blinders that they put on themselves, they never attempt to do what they really would like to do.

To help them over that hurdle so that they can begin to dream, I frequently use this exercise. I ask them to look around the room and choose an object in the room. Once they have chosen a particular object, I ask, "Did you know that at one time that object was no more than an idea in someone's mind?"

Everything that exists was, at one time, nothing more than a concept or an idea in someone's imagination. The same thing is true of an identity. If we can imagine all of our strengths and characteristics that make us uniquely us and fantasize a role in which those would be used, that may very well be the beginning of the creation of that role.

A minister's wife needs to come to the church that employs her husband with her head on her shoulders, knowing who she is, and not being influenced by her predecessors or by others' expectations. Knowing who you are is a lifelong journey in personal growth and self-awareness and self-love. If you enter a church environment that way, you are going to be effective in whatever role you and God find for you.

The first few times you encounter an expectation that doesn't feel comfortable or doesn't fit, you need to choose the behavior that is healthy for you. Some person or little group in the church may be disappointed, even shocked, but they will survive and they will get to know you as a happy, fulfilled person.

But, if you try to fit into everything that is already there and try to please everybody and it doesn't fit you, anger and resentment will build up as time goes on. You will begin to withdraw more and more.

The best course of action from the beginning is to find your God-given identity and be true to it. You will be happier, your husband will be happier, and ultimately the church will be happier and will respect you as a model.

It is my fondest wish that God's children be happy.
I don't mean ecstatic or continually exuberant;
    I mean happy, full of joy,
    that deep-down contentment that persists
    even in the midst of trials and tribulations
    and difficult circumstances.
As the very children of God,
    we really don't have a thing to worry about.
Whatever our real needs,
    we know that God will fulfill them in His own time
    and in accordance with His will.
We can well afford to celebrate,
    to live in thankfulness,
    and to allow the incomprehensible peace of God
    to mend the frayed edges of our troubled lives
    and make us serene and secure in our Christian faith.
                —Philippians 4, *Epistles/Now*

11
Spiritual Life Is Not the Same as Church Life

Feeling the pain and hurt resulting from the forced termination was what I wanted to avoid. I was not trying to avoid the presence of God. However, that is what happened. I could not feel God's presence.

Where was God? How could God leave us out on this limb to take care of ourselves? How could this be God's church and people be so cruel? How could God bless this church? If God calls us and sends us on a mission, how can one or a few individuals call it off? What is the sense in all this?

Question after question ran through my mind as I tried to sort through what was happening and what it meant in light of all I had believed about God.

We are taught to believe that God is always in control. From my perspective, that simply was not true in this situation. Human beings took the control from God. So, where is God? What does He intend to do about all this?

I walked through the rooms of our house, thinking and crying. For endless hours I sat at the piano, playing, and crying, crying, crying. One song in particular, "There's a Wideness in God's Mercy," meant so much to me. My prayer was, "God, I really want to believe that."

When I am healthy emotionally, a need for time alone for Scripture and prayer, a time for devotions, is always with me.

However, in the wake of forced termination, I had no desire to do these things that were a normal part of my spiritual life. I just felt nothing, as if God weren't there.

Working through those feelings is difficult, but necessary. I had to separate what had happened at the church from my own spiritual relationship to God. All of my activities had so surrounded the church that I began to realize that perhaps my spiritual life had been mixed up with and intertwined with church activities. The church had become my spiritual life.

A crisis such as forced termination makes you reevaluate what you were doing all this for in the first place. My whole life has been so absorbed by the church that I had not stopped to think what church is all about. Why do we even have church? I had to get it all in perspective.

Realizing this even caused me to question my husband about his motivations for standing in front of the church conducting the music every Sunday. "Why do you direct the choir? Is it for your self-gratification? Your being in control? Hearing beautiful music?" These things have nothing to do with our spiritual life, but many of us forget that.

Such heartbreak pushes one into a sea of confusion with questions of all sorts swimming around. You can begin to doubt almost everything you've thought was true.

Of course, God had not abandoned us. I was just so devastated by the forced termination that I felt deserted by God. But, God is not the church. My relationship to Him is not dependent upon the church, and especially not upon only one church.

Once again, Frank was an example for me. As he and I talked, week after week, trying to make sense out of all this, he said the only conclusion that he could come to was that God is sovereign, and we do not question a sovereign God. We do what there is to do each day. He reassured me and pointed out that men had done this thing; God did not do it.

Frank believed that if God intended to open another door for us, He would. Conversely, if He didn't intend to open another door, He wouldn't. Frank has admitted that, for him, when prayers aren't answered and direction is not given, he has to be careful to not doubt a lot of things about God. But, Frank also believes in getting up and doing what has to be done each day. It helps one get through the days until the direction and answers do come. And that is what he did.

Another thing which helped me was a poem by Lois Cheney:

fifty

Once I saw a little boy proudly show his mother a painting he'd made at school. She looked at it, and turned it this way and that and looked some more. "It's lovely," she murmured. Suddenly, she exclaimed, "Oh! I see what it is! It's a house and a tree, and there's a big sun, and . . . ." The little boy grabbed the paper and bunching it all up, he hollered,

THAT'S NOT WHAT IT MEANT!

Did you ever, oh so carefully, lay out just how things were and how they worked, and why they worked, and then sat back satisfied? Then you heard someone repeat what you'd said, oh so carefully, and you hardly recognized it, and your brain screamed,

THAT'S NOT WHAT I MEANT!

Did you ever pry out of your heart, your mind, a tiny nugget of how you truly felt, and then told someone, probably someone special, then stared in disbelief as he responded wrong, all wrong, and your every pore shouted,

THAT'S NOT WHAT I MEANT!

Sometimes, smug times
When I'm talking about God
When I'm praying about God
When I'm working for God,
Sometimes, smug times
When I'm very busy

in the church
about the church
around the church
I wonder
if God isn't
sighing,
or whispering,
or saying,
or hollering,
THAT'S NOT WHAT I MEANT![1]

My attitude toward the church, I believe, is healthier right now than it has ever been. My relationship to God is not dependent on my church involvement. In other words, I do not equate my spiritual life with "much activity and acceptance down at the church." Those of us whose lives have been so wrapped up in church activities, frequently for many years, need to untangle ourselves and step back far enough—and long enough—to be sure our own relationship to God is the central point for our church activity. I have grown into a healthy dependence on God and have come to realize that He is always with me.

In all of my wandering and questioning, one thing came to me as if God were talking to me, directly and audibly, "Oh Myra, what have I promised you?"

There is not one tangible thing that God has promised me. He didn't say, "I'll give you a house (or whatever)."

He just said, "I'll take care of you."

He promised to be my strength, my Comforter. But, they're not tangible.

He promised to supply my needs. I don't know what form that will be. It may be an emotional need. It may be a physical need.

I kept praying, "God, give Frank another job." And, I had

my own concept of what that ought to be. God didn't promise that. God didn't promise He would give Frank another church. That may not be a great revelation for other people, but it was for me.

The most marvelous thing is that here we are, several years after the forced termination, and we are all right. Not every day has been easy, some days were better than others, and some have been absolutely wonderful. We have been able to make it. God has cared for us, and we know it.

Others' Stories

"At these difficult times, I have concentrated on just reading Scripture," says Susan, "and letting the Word of God penetrate my mind. *God's Promises of Life*, a book given to us by friends, has Scripture passages dealing with anger, depression, suffering, praise, and so forth. The Bible speaks to my needs as I read. My prayer has been simply, "Lord, help. Give us direction. Show us you still care about us." The Lord has given assurance of His care through people who have encouraged us with kind words and their promise of prayer. The only way I ever came out of this hole (of depression) was that God didn't let me go."

"The loving Father who led us up to the point of dismissal is still the same loving Father who holds the future. After all, God did not fail us, people did. Turning to the Father for comfort and guidance is a must if one is ever to be restored," says Mary. "He never fails, and He will never ask for our resignation! God still loves us with His everlasting love."

"I remain confident," says Naomi, "that God has a plan for us and in His own time will reveal it to us. I know that time will heal some of the hurt, and I just pray that He will help us overcome our impatience and give us understanding of why this had to take place in our lives."

"Through all of this," says Lucille, "we have not given up. Our faith is strong. My husband is active in church; we all are. He is singing in a choir, he leads when asked, and he supplies when he can."

"The only thing I am really sure of is God's unfailing love for me and mine for Him," declares Jackie.

"Last week during one of my depression days," says Annie, "I sat praying, or attempting to pray, and thought, *Why do I keep praying? God isn't hearing me. My prayers aren't even going as high as the ceiling.* I have had this thought many times before, but suddenly this thought came to mind (I know it was put there by the Holy Spirit): *Your prayers don't have to go above the ceiling. God is everywhere. He is right here beside you. The Holy Spirit is sealed within you, interceding for you when you don't even know how to pray, when you have reached the place you feel you have said all you can but with no results.*

"I then read Romans 8:26-27: 'In the same way, the Spirit helps us in our weakness. We do not know what we ought to pray for, but the Spirit himself intercedes for us with groans that words cannot express. And he who searches our hearts knows the mind of the Spirit, because the Spirit intercedes for the saints in accordance with God's will' (NIV).

"I know I am a long way from being what God wants me to be," continues Annie. "I have not done everything He wanted me to do, nor always lived an exemplary life. I've failed God many times, in many ways. I have to ask His forgiveness daily and over and over for the same things. I have not found complete peace, have not accepted the situation without question, but I feel closer to God now, more at peace than I did before all this happened. In many ways I'm a stronger Christian, and I believe some day God is going to provide us with the place of service He is preparing for us. Psalm 138:7-8: 'Though I am surrounded by troubles, you will bring me safely through them. You will clench your fist against my angry enemies! Your power will save me. The Lord will work out his plans for my life' "(TLB).

Dan's Observations

Naturally, many of the things we've discussed already bear directly or indirectly on the whole area of one's spiritual life. Separating one's spiritual life from the life of the church may be especially difficult for a minister's family.

But, you need to try to do that. Sometimes we get on the train and we ride and ride. Occasionally, we need to stop, get off, and ask, "Where are we going? Why are we on this train and who said we should be on it in the first place?"

Some Christians may mistakenly identify their own will, their own choices, and their own decisions as being God's will. God's will is a very difficult thing to determine. When is it God and when is it me? When are my decisions and the things I'm choosing directed, at a subconscious level, out of my personal needs, my selfishness? And when does God use my own thinking processes to come to a decision that He is leading me to make? It is very difficult to separate clearly our voice from the voice of God.

Another thing ministers have to face, and this too poses a serious danger for them, is the tendency to speak for God so frequently from the pulpit that they lose the capacity to separate when they are talking and when they are being prophetic and speaking for God. It's dangerous. This very matter can shake the integrity of a minister who loses touch with his own human

needs and human decisions and describes them as God speaking
to or through him.

I say this in order to make a significant point about the forced
termination experience. Once we are in a termination situation,
if we truly believe God led us to this church and now we are
being terminated, do we define everything that happens to us as
God's will? If so, then we do have to blame God with the fact
that we are losing our job.

If, however, we believe God moves in our lives in ways that
many times we do not even understand until perhaps years
later, we then have a different view of the termination. We then
follow and keep in perspective our own abilities, our own skills,
and the direction that these will take us, knowing that God
works in very natural and normal processes. We believe that
God inspires us to move in certain directions sometimes, but
never directing us to act in conflict with our ability.

In other words, there are several options as we talk about
God's role in this termination.

First of all, it could be that God did indeed lead us to this
position and that God is indeed using this termination as a
method of redirecting our lives.

Secondly, it could be that God led us to this position and has
nothing to do with this termination, but human beings are acting out of touch with God's will. In that event, rather than to
hold anger and hostility toward those people who are not understanding God's will and God's way, remember the life of
Joseph, which we discussed earlier. Recall that frequently
things turned against him, and yet frequently God used those
negative events in his life to bring about a greater opportunity
of service.

In my life when I believe someone wished me ill or acted in
an adversarial fashion toward me, I cannot recall one time when
I have not benefited from it. In each case God has shown me a

better way to serve or has given me both comfort and redirection. So, whatever another person's action against me, the outcome has been positive.

In many ways it really doesn't matter whether a church is doing the right thing or not in terminating a minister. The only thing that matters is whether or not this minister and his family are in tune with God enough to know that whatever the future holds, "I know who holds the future."

If God holds my future in His hands, what can a church do? They will only do things that God will, in time, use to bless me and to enable me to bless others.

A third option to consider is the possibility that you should have never gone to this church in the first place, that God may not have been in it at all. If that's the case, it means you are human, that you've made a mistake. But if you made that mistake, now it is being rectified, and it offers you the opportunity to do something that God does want you to do.

The biggest mistake you can make is to blame God for what is happening. God does not impose His will on individuals whom He has made free. He does not give us the capacity to choose or to not choose Him, to follow or not follow Him, and then turn around and force His will on us. It is inconsistent; it is inconceivable that God would give us such freedom and then impose His will on us.

God has told us from the beginning that if we want to make a fool out of ourselves, if we want to ignore all of His guidelines and live our lives based on what we think is right instead of what He has shown us through the lives of the biblical characters and the life of Jesus Christ, He'll let us do it. The same goes for the church. If church members want to ignore everything God is about and all the principles He has taught through the Bible, He will let them do it.

So why be mad at God because human beings have made a

choice? If human beings in a church are making such a choice, and it is God's will, believe me in the long run we want that. If human beings in God's church are making a bad decision that is against God's will, then ultimately the same God who gives them the freedom to make that choice will take care of us and provide for us. If that is the case, those human beings need our prayers, not our hostility, and our forgiveness, not our hatred.

Notice, I am not saying God will provide you another place of service, nor can I say your experience will not harm you. The whole message of Job is that we don't have any guarantees or particulars, but we do know God will care for us. And that is enough. We move ahead, believing.

We have wept and whined long enough.
It is time we claim God's proffered gifts
   and begin to act responsively
   as His divinely endowed servants.
Whereas we, as fallible human beings,
      may claim the right to be imperfect,
      we have, as well, the responsibility to focus
      upon God's goals for our lives
      and to become more and more
      like the Christ who brought us to our God.
                              —Philippians 2, *Epistles/Now*

12
The Next Church,
The Next Job

Unfortunately for most forced termination victims, the next church is not the next job. Many of these people find themselves in situations similar to ours. The immediate need is for survival.

We took a second mortgage on our house, and Frank took part-time and odd jobs. Although I was working, my income alone would not support us.

We have talked with other people who had no debts other than their monthly bills. But, even when people are in fairly good financial condition, they have to cut corners, and savings may be depleted. Other people have had medical problems or concerns that were expensive.

No matter what the person's financial status at the time of termination, finding another job soon is a necessity.

During this time of searching and trying to find a permanent job, Frank and I talked a lot about why he wanted so badly to be a minister of music for a church. So strong is his desire to serve as a minister of music that he has commented that he felt he was "born" to minister. This calling has never left him.

Eventually, six months after the termination, he found full-time employment in a music-related field, and he threw himself into that job with the same determination he does everything else. Colleagues in the church music ministry were the ones who recommended Frank for this job. There are people who can and who will help, and they are healers.

Our family went in three different directions for church. Our daughter continued going to our former church. Frank supplied and had some interim positions. As I mentioned, attending our former church with my daughter became impossible for me. Unable to worship, I knew I was only hurting myself further so I found other places to attend worship services. But, for a while none of us were really serving in a church together and, certainly, not in the manner in which we were accustomed.

Frank was called to a church in our denomination on a part-time basis. We've learned that many forced termination victims join other denominations and serve through them because they are unable to find employment within their own. So we were fortunate at that point.

Also, getting another church position is difficult when one has no current church position. Two pastors told Frank, "We would love to have you, but cannot ask our church to consider an unemployed minister of music."

The church that did employ him was small, so small that the choir had no place to sit as a group, but had to sit with the rest of the congregation. Each section of the choir had only a few people in it. Seeing my husband directing that small choir in that small church was difficult for me. At first, I sat watching him, through tears, and could only remember the former "glories" of the big choirs and big programs he used to conduct.

Prior to this, Frank had always been on the staff of large churches with 4,000 to 7,200 members and church music programs involving 600 to 900 people. The smallest staff on which he had ever served was one with fifteen people.

A friend of ours in that church told me something that I've thought a lot about. She said that the important thing might not be the size of the group with which we were working, but the individual lives we are able to influence and to whom we can minister. From time to time, I've thought about that, and Frank and I have talked a lot about those individuals in our ministry. Considering one's ministry to individuals sheds new light on size.

Also, at first, I had that old feeling that everyone in the church knew who we were, what we had done, and why we were at their church. But, they didn't.

This church, and we are still serving there, turned out to be one of the healing forces in our lives. I remember one touch of sensitivity from the pastor, a loving man, when we first went there. The Sunday we joined the church, he did not ask us to come forward to the front of the church, which is the custom in our denomination. I do not think I could have walked from my pew down the aisle. Even though the church is very small that aisle seemed very long back then. I simply was not strong enough. But, I had found a place that would let me be me, and I didn't have to feel guilty about it!

Although the choir knew nothing of what we had been through, their support and their responsiveness to Frank's leadership have been crucial to our healing. They have been so appreciative of the quality of Frank's work.

Also, the preaching has been superb, and the sermons at this church spoke to me. Another factor in my healing was the strong Christians who were already members of this church. Their spiritual depth ministered to us, and they allowed us to heal without us—especially me—having to be "leaders" immediately.

This church continues to grow, both in numbers and in size of the building. We now have an appropriate place for the choir during the services. The pastors have been people with whom we could worship and grow spiritually. And the people are supportive and participate in the choir program.

Although he admits he could spend the entire week at his part-time job, Frank now says he has the best of both worlds.

For my part, I love playing for the services at this church. Frank's choice of music; the dear, dedicated, and committed pianist; and the loving choir members all make it enjoyable. I now look forward to choir rehearsal for the first time in my memory.

Others' Stories

"Our family has since become a part of a new nondenominational church begun shortly after all of this happened where my husband is the music director," says Jackie, "but we desire to be back in a Southern Baptist church as soon as possible and are earnestly seeking such a position."

"We went through the process of trying to find another church. He still hasn't given up on that," says Lucille. "But, we knew he had to find a job. He had always been interested in investments so he started studying to become a financial planner. There are days when he enjoys it, but most days he leaves down, because he doesn't have a church."

"The pastor told my husband the church could no longer pay him after the first of June and handed a typed resignation to him to sign, stating the resignation was to take effect immediately," says Annie. "A resource person in our denomination recommended he sign or he would have trouble getting another church.

"It seems there should be some way men who have been through forced terminations, especially when it is the result of a few people within a church who have been responsible and not the staff member's fault, can be brought before churches in need of their skills and the skills of their wives and their families. How do you go about letting it be known that you have been terminated through no fault of your own and you are seeking another church? How do you present your experience without sounding like you are all-righteous and the other people involved are all sinners? Without belittling them?

"This is a high unemployment area, and there are no jobs for either of us," continues Annie. "When we moved here, we thought we would stay until we were ready to retire, so we bought our home. We have had it on the market for over ten months and have had very few inquiries and no offers at all. We can't go off and leave it since we invested all our savings in it. My husband's sixty-second birthday was in May, so he applied for early retirement. He receives $460 per month. A small church called him as interim music director and pays him $35 per week, making an income of $600. Our tithe, house payment, and health insurance costs $690 per month. We praise the Lord that each month from somewhere—a little from friends and relatives, a revival, etc.—enough has come in to pay utilities, gas for the car to go to church, and for food. God didn't say He would give us great wealth, just that He would supply our needs. We have some bills that have had to go unpaid, but we have explained to our creditors that we will pay them as soon as we sell the house or get a job. I really dislike having unpaid bills.

"I began Bible studies after the initial shock wore off to prepare for the next assignment God has for us. . . . I want to be prepared for whatever God has for us to do, whenever He is ready, and if He decides not to use us in this capacity again, at least it has helped me to grow," concludes Annie.

"I have so much to rejoice over, so much to be thankful for," exclaims Justine. "We have just celebrated our first anniversary in our new church. The church honored us with a reception and a love offering of $2,500. They are a loving, caring church led by a wise, loving pastor. I feel as though we've been led right into the promised land.

"I cannot begin to tell you the many ways the Lord worked in our lives. And now to be serving in a church that is so God-loving. I sometimes am overwhelmed by His goodness! I still have some of the same problems that I did before the termination. I've also become more inward. It'll be a long time before I'll be able to open up to people, to let people know the 'real' Justine.

"Our story has a happy ending, but I know many terminated couples in our former state who are still in the valley."

"We are going Sunday in view of a call," says Lisa. "This continues to be very difficult for me. I thought I would be very excited when this time came. I can't say that I am. I'm very surprised that I can feel such peace about another church and yet feel sick at the same time. My head says this is right one minute; the next minute I'm at the point of tears.

"I believe Mark and I both should be back serving in a church, but I'm very scared. I want this only if it is what God wants."

"From the largest church in the state, we now serve in the smallest," points out Carolyn.

"The forced termination made me withdraw from church people. I just didn't want to trust them," says Beth. "I have to admit that after eight months in our new church, I tend to keep my distance. The forced termination experience left me feeling insecure.

"We are now at a great church. They know what we have been through. They are loving, letting us be ourselves. They give us the leeway to hear us when things go wrong. They are very loving. Couldn't be better.

"When I think about the past, I don't think I could do it as well as I did the first time. Now, I just want peace, quiet, and for people to get along. I think, with time, I'll heal. Even now, I just have to work through it," concludes Beth.

"As we look back over the one year and two months at this church, we can see trouble from the beginning," explains Susan. "The previous minister of education had been asked to resign also. But, my husband believed the pastor when he told him the previous minister of education had just not done his job. This was our first mistake. We should have ended contact with this pastor when we found out about the previous minister of education. Two other staff members had recently resigned with short terms (we didn't know this until after we moved) and another staff member resigned shortly after we arrived on the field. In the future we will call previous staff members and check references of the pastor thoroughly, something we haven't done in the past.

"For four months after the forced termination, my husband did not want to go back into a church staff position. We both have a deep sense of calling and today we are seeking to serve the Lord. We hope and pray that someday we will be back where we know we belong."

"We are struggling with reorganizing our lives at the present time," says Naomi. "We have just recently purchased our first house and we want to stay in this community. Two of our children have married and live here; the other lives only an hour away, and after all these years, this is home to us.

"We also feel that with another full-time church at this point of our lives, we would probably have to face termination again very soon because of our age. We definitely are trying to follow the Lord's leadership in this matter and not put our selfish desires first. It has been three months since my husband resigned, and he has not been able to find satisfactory employment up until this time. I have held a full-time position in the school system for fifteen years and am still in my position.

"We struggle with impatience, wanting an opportunity to open up right now. We are now in the process of talking to a church of another denomination about a part-time position. We are praying that this will work out, but again we are dealing with our own impatience rather than waiting on the Lord."

Dan's Observations

"You won't have any trouble finding another church" is a myth. Forced termination victims frequently hear this from well-meaning friends and family, but it just isn't necessarily so.

Finding another church, when you are not already on a staff, is difficult. Remember that I talked about the stigma attached to a minister who has been forced to leave a church? This is one of them. People are suspicious, and there is really no way of supplying them with the truth.

We talked with one family in which the man was being considered for a position on another staff. When he was forced to terminate his current church, the prospective church dropped negotiations and the pastor made the comment that this "is definitely a stumbling block" for that man to join his church's staff.

I do not have the statistics to prove this, but I suspect that most forced termination victims do not go to another church staff. If they do, it may not be within their own denomination.

Because some sort of employment is needed, many will take almost any job. You may want to do that just to meet your financial obligations while, at the same time, preparing for and searching for a more permanent position or a new career.

But, you will want to find another church in which to worship

as quickly as possible. Depending on where you live, this may
be difficult. A small town may not offer many opportunities.
But, when you do go to worship, beware of the tendency to
relive the pain of the past. You will be tempted, while sitting in
the congregation, to remember. Every person who leads a part
of the service in some way will remind you of what used to be,
what you or your spouse used to do. Certain hymns will evoke
memories that can be painful.

This will be less of a problem if you have handled the termination and grief process well.

I would like to make one significant point about moving on
to the next church or the next job. It is important to go into
whatever position, circumstance, or opportunity you have with
the intent and determination to do well. This is especially important when you perceive this new position to be a step down
or not as significant as the one you were forced to leave.

Many times, out of anger and out of depression, we begrudg-
ingly accept new assignments and do not do them well. My
strong recommendation to you is that you, as the old saying
goes, "Bloom where you are planted." If God gives you a place
of responsibility, the task should be done well.

More than once I have seen a situation that appeared to be
abysmal, with no opportunity for growth or progress, turn out
to be the foundation for a whole new world. It is almost as if
God put these people in a certain position as a means of giving
them the opportunity to recover, to do a good job, and to move
on.

Understand your denominational and local church polity.
We pointed out earlier that the churches that practice a congregational form of church polity are more susceptible to forced
termination problems. In this form of church government, the
members of the congregation make the decisions about church
business. With no official hierarchy of control, misunderstand-

ings in the area of hiring and firing can happen more easily.

If and when you do accept a position on another church staff, don't be naive. Know what you are getting into. It is all right, even a good thing, for you to ask questions. Ask all the questions you need until you feel sure you understand this particular church.

Who has the power to hire and fire in this church?

For what reason could you be fired? How are performance reviews handled? Who gives them? When? Many people now consider the employment practices of churches to be similar to those of businesses, and businesses increasingly are having to meet certain regulations in their firing or dismissal procedures.

Study the church bylaws and minutes of business meetings.

What does the church or staff expect of the minister's spouse?

Be open and forthright with the church concerning your expectations.

Investigate the history of the church and the pastor's relationship with former staff members.

You might want to consider requesting a written contract of employment. You may feel a contract is too businesslike in a spiritual institution, but it may clarify issues and be good for the minister and the church. You will have written down what you can expect from the church and what they can expect from you.

You can move ahead, going to another church, still believing in the God who calls you, but also being more in control of your own life and future.

Epilogue

Where am I today? I asked my pastor, Dr. Kenny Cooper, who has known me only after our forced termination, to tell you where he sees me today.

He observes, "Myra has learned pain management; not pain alleviation. She is involved, but not so involved that she can't back away. She has reinvested her talents in ministry and other outlets. Myra finds therapy through helping others. Her work at the Sunday School Board and the writing of this book are examples of the way she is investing herself in ministry.

"Myra shows a dependence on God which is evident to me in her language. She has worked through a lot of anger, but it is an on-going process as things may trigger old feelings. Myra is sensitive to the vulnerability of the ministry and is finding a ministry of encouraging other wives in the ministry.

"She has experienced complete brokenness and humiliation. That is not a thing a person can forgive and forget, and then it's over with. It has to be dealt with again and again. I see Myra as a person who is doing just that."

My pastor is correct. I deal daily with the aftermath of forced termination. Never do I want you to think getting over forced termination is a one-time event or that it is easy. I make a conscious decision each day that I will make it.

The shattering of our lives moved me from humiliation to

dignity. When termination smashed our lives into pieces, I had to realize what was left. That was my relationship with God, my family, and a new ministry with talents and abilities that I'm developing and using.

The journey continues. I am moving beyond the termination. I know that you can, too. You have God-given resources within you and around you. You have a steadfast God who loves you.

Sharing all of this so that I might minister to others is the purpose for this book. My prayer is that it offers you significant help and reassures you that I know, I care, I encourage you, and you have my prayers. Our shattered lives can be put back together, redesigned into beautiful, new pictures of God's creation.

Notes

Chapter 1

1. A popular belief is that a psychosomatic illness is "all in your head," and if you really wanted to be well you could be. That is, if you just wanted to be badly enough. Dan gave me a correct definition of psychosomatic: psycho = mind; somatic = body/physical. When we say psychosomatic, we mean that the mind—because of conclusions, attitudes, and positions the mind has taken about life and the mind's inflexibility to adapt to reality—produces an illness that is real. It can produce an organic change and a chemical change in the body that over time can result in things such as ulcers, migraines, backaches, and respiratory and digestive problems. Dan has told me that I had a genetic predisposition to certain physical problems, but the stress—which is produced by the expectations, the conclusions in the mind, and the inability to flex those in the face of reality—activated the weakest part of my system.

Chapter 2

1. J. Courtney Silvy, "Let's Run Off the Preacher!" *Baptist Program*, October 1981, 20.

2. _____, "Our Readers Speak Their Minds," *Baptist Program*, June/July 1987, 4.

3. Brooks Faulkner, *Forced Termination* (Nashville: Broadman Press, 1986), 8.

4. Louis Ball, "A Study of Tenure for the Minister of Music at a Time of Pastoral Change." Reprinted by permission from *Ex-Pastors: Why Men Leave the Parish Ministry*, by Gerald J. Jud, Edgar W. Mills, Jr., and Genevieve Walters Burch. Copyright 1970, United Church Press, New York, N.Y.

5. Gerald J. Jud, Edgar W. Mills, Jr., and Genevieve Walters Burch, *Ex-Pastors: Why Men Leave the Parish Ministry* (Philadelphia/Boston: The Pilgrim Press, 1970), 94. Used by permission.

6. Tommy D. Bledsoe, "Responses Vary When Church Staffer Fired," *The Christian Index*, 12 March 1981, 4.

7. Ibid.

8. "Outplacement Counseling Need Noted for Fired Ministers," *The Christian Index*, 26 March 1981, 9.

9. "Church Reaction Important to Families of Ministers," *The Christian Index*, 19 March 1981, 3.

10. Speed Leas, "A Study of Involuntary Terminations in Some Presbyterian, Episcopal and United Church of Christ Congregations" (The Alban Institute, 1980), 16.

11. Ibid, 22.

Chapter 3

1. Alan Richman with Cable Neuhouse, "Up From Olympus," *People Weekly*, 25 July 1988, 38.

Chapter 7

1. Nick Stinnett and John DeFrain, *Secrets of Strong Families* (New York: Berkeley Books, 1986), 14.

2. Kent and Barbara Hughes, *Liberating Ministry from the Success Syndrome* (Tyndale House Publishers, 1987). Used by permission of Tyndale House Publishers, Inc. All rights reserved.

Chapter 8

1. Virginia McAffee, "Pastor's Wives Need Help, Too!" *Baptist Program*, October 1987, 18.

Chapter 9

1. Lewis B. Smedes, *Forgive and Forget: Healing the Hurts We Don't Deserve.* (New York: Pocket Books, 1984), 170.

2. Ibid., 12.

Chapter 11

1. Lois A. Cheney, *God Is No Fool* (Nashville: Abingdon Press), 93-94. Used by permission.

Bibliography

Ball, Louis. "A Study of Tenure for the Minister of Music at a Time of Pastoral Change." Jefferson City, Tenn.: Carson-Newman College, 1983. This study offers significant comments on the effects of forced termination on families.

Bledsoe, Tommy Dalton. "Case Studies of Georgia Baptist Ministerial Families Who Have Resigned Pastorates Without Immediate Prospects for Another Pastorate." Atlanta: Georgia State University, 1980.

Burns, David D. *Feeling Good*. New York: Signet Books, 1980. This book introduces the principles of Cognitive Therapy, which teaches that by changing the way we think we can alter our moods, deal with emotional problems, and get rid of depression without the use of drugs.

Carter, Jimmy and Rosalyn. *Everything to Gain*. New York: Random House, 1987. This is an excellent book for people who have their own personal dreams canceled and must seek other avenues for service and a fulfilling life. The Carters tell about ways they have involved themselves in meaningful work and offer suggestions others may use.

Faulkner, Brooks R. *Forced Termination*. Nashville: Broadman Press, 1986. Subtitled "Redemptive Options for Ministers and Churches," the book is written by a person actively involved in ministering to people forced to terminate.

Grubbs, Bruce. *The First Two Years*. Nashville: Convention Press, 1979. This step-by-step guide will help pastors as they begin work in a new church. It covers areas many ministers may not normally consider as significant.

Jud, Gerald J.; Mills, Edgar W.; and Burch, Genevieve Walters. *Ex-Pastors. Why Men Leave the Parish Ministry*. New York, Boston: Pilgrim Press, 1970. This book looks at the problem and offers suggestions for improvement. Contains information on wives and families as they relate to the ministry.

Kubler-Ross, Elisabeth. *On Death and Dying*. New York: Macmillan, 1969. This well-known book covers the stages of grief.

Leas, Speed. "A Study of Involuntary Terminations in Some Presbyterian, Episcopal, and United Church of Christ Congregations." Washington, D.C.: The Alban Institute, 1980.

Mace, David and Vera. Any of their books on marriage are excellent for couples seeking a deeper, more intimate relationship, as well as surviving and growing through a crisis.

McGee, Dan, *ABC's of Stress*. Arlington, Tex.: Metro-McGee Associates, 1989. A curriculum manual written for mental health professionals for use in psychiatric hospitals. A complete description of the author's cognitive-behavioral model for stress management is included.

Rainey, Dennis and Barbara. *Building Your Mate's Self-Esteem*. San Bernardino: Here's Life Publishers, 1986. A graduate of Dallas Theological Seminary, Rainey is the national director of the Family Ministry of Campus Crusade for Christ. He and Barbara have spoken at more than one hundred family life conferences.

Smith, Nancy Calvert. *Journey Out of Nowhere*. Waco: Word, Inc., 1973. This first-person account of a young woman's mental breakdown and recovery shows what can happen when one imposes unrealistic expectations on oneself.

Smedes, Lewis B. *Forgive and Forget*. New York: Pocket Books, 1984. Subtitled "Healing the Hurts We Don't Deserve," this book is written from a Christian perspective.

Stinnett, Nick and DeFrain, John. *Secrets of Strong Families*. New York: Berkley Books, 1986. This book grew out of a research project conducted by college professors. It contains the six qualities of strong families, one of which is spiritual wellness.

Veninga, Robert L. *A Gift of Hope*. New York: Ballentine Books, 1985. Subtitled "How We Survive Our Tragedies," this book is a good resource written from a secular perspective.

The Authors

MYRA McGEE MARSHALL experienced forced termination when her husband was forced to resign his position as a minister of music on a church staff. Her story provides the basis for this book. In addition to being the wife of a man who has served more than twenty-five years as a Southern Baptist minister of music, she is a musician and the daughter of a Southern Baptist minister.

Mrs. Marshall has led Southern Baptist state and associational preschool music clinics in Georgia, Alabama, Texas, Louisiana, Arkansas, Missouri, and Tennessee, and has led music leadership conferences at Glorieta and Ridgecrest Baptist Conference Centers for the Church Music Department of the Baptist Sunday School Board.

She has written preschool music curriculum and children's Sunday School curriculum for the Sunday School Board. Marshall set up and taught music curriculum for church day-care centers for six years. She has been a church organist or pianist since she was twelve years old.

Marshall is on the editorial staff for children's Sunday School material at the Sunday School Board and is a free-lance makeup artist for the Baptist Telecommunication Network (BTN). She is also a fashion and wardrobe consultant.

Marshall lives with her husband in Franklin, Tennessee. Both are members of Bellevue Baptist Church, Nashville, where he is minister of music. She is the mother of two and the grandmother of five.

DAN McGEE, Ph.D., is a medical psychotherapist best known for his research and clinical work in stress management. He provides the expert's advice and counsel in this book. As the brother of Mrs. Marshall, he is intimately aware of her story. A marriage and family therapist with a private practice in the Dallas-Fort Worth area since 1975, he is also certified at the highest level in pain management. As a therapist, a minister's son, and an ordained minister for eighteen years before entering the mental health field, he offers insight and professional help for those experiencing forced termination.

Dr. McGee is a graduate of Baylor University, Southwestern Baptist Theological Seminary, Texas Woman's University and did additional graduate work at the University of Texas at Arlington. His church-related work experience included the pastorate, youth and music ministry, denominational work and education ministry in large urban churches. He has written curriculum for the Sunday School Board. In one of his denominational roles, he frequently became a counselor to ministers and was active in the process of helping churches secure ministers and handle situations where termination was inevitable. He is presently a deacon at First Baptist Church, Arlington, Texas.

McGee is president and owner of two corporations. Metro-McGee Associates, Inc., is a mental health consulting firm providing inpatient services in private psychiatric hospitals, and consulting and training programs for small and large corporations. Metro Counseling Associates, Inc., is a counseling center with a multiprofessional staff representing psychiatry, clinical psychology, marriage and family therapy, sex therapy, clinical social work, chemical dependency, therapy and medical psychology and psychotherapy for pre-adolescents and adults.

In addition to private practice and consulting work, McGee conducts group stress therapy several hours a week at the Psychiatric Institute of Fort Worth. He appears weekly on COPE, a national one-hour live call-in television show on the ACTS Satellite Network, Inc. His published work includes two audiocassettes, *ABC's of Stress* and *Talking Through a Panic Attack*, plus curriculum guides used in psychiatric hospitals. Currently he is writing a book on the use of his ABC Stress Management model. Frequently interviewed by newspaper, magazine, and television reporters, McGee is a well-known conference leader and speaker in fields of stress and family life.

His national and international certifications include:

Fellow and Diplomate, American Board of Medical Psychotherapists;

Diplomate, International Academy of Behavioral Medicine Counseling and Psychotherapy, Inc.;

Clinical Member, American Association for Marriage and Family Therapy;

Certified Sex Therapist, American Association of Sex Educators, Counselors and Therapists, Inc.;

Diplomate, American Academy of Pain Management;

Diplomate, American Board of Sexology;

Board Certified, National Board for Certified Counselors, Inc.

McGee is married to the former Sandra Wheeler of Jonesboro, Arkansas, who has been a homemaker, public-school teacher, and corporate financial officer. They are the parents of two daughters.

JENNIFER BRYON OWEN worked with Mrs. Marshall on the book's design and content. Mrs. Owen, also the daughter of a Southern Baptist minister, attended Mississippi College, and received her degree in journalism and English from the University of Mississippi where she also has done graduate study in mass communications. She has been a publicity copywriter for Broadman Press and a communications specialist for the Book Store Division, both of the Baptist Sunday School Board. She also has been products group manager for Woman's Missionary Union, SBC, as well as owning her own public relations and marketing firm.

Now a full-time writer, Owen's book, *Quiet Moments for a New Mother*, was published by New Hope (Birmingham, Ala.) in 1987. She is the author of the 1990 Adult Home Mission Study book published by the Home Mission Board, wrote the script for the accompanying videotape, as well as writing the accompanying Teaching Guide, published by Woman's Missionary Union. Her articles have been published in *Writer's Digest*, *Christian Life*, *Christian Retailing* (contributing editor), *Christian Bookseller*, *Bookstore Journal*, *Charisma*, *Christian Single*, *Church Administration*, *Mature Living*, *Royal Service*, *Spectrum*, *Adventure*, *encounter!*, *Alive Now!*, *event*, *The Church Musician*, *The Washington Star*, *The Daily Mississippian*, *The Jackson Daily News*, *The Upper Room Consumer Catalog*, and *Fishing Tackle Trade News*.

She is a member of Women in Communications, a member and former president of Baptist Public Relations Association, a member and former Nashville chapter president of the Religious Public Relations Council, and is on the board of advisers for the Georgia Freelance Writers Association.

Owen lives with her husband and son in Roswell, Georgia, and is a member of the Northside Drive Baptist Church in Atlanta.